Harry Woodworth Huntington

My Dog and I

Being a concise Treatise of the various Breeds of Dogs, their Origin and Uses

Harry Woodworth Huntington

My Dog and I
Being a concise Treatise of the various Breeds of Dogs, their Origin and Uses

ISBN/EAN: 9783337143312

Printed in Europe, USA, Canada, Australia, Japan

Cover: Foto ©ninafisch / pixelio.de

More available books at **www.hansebooks.com**

MY DOG AND I

BEING A CONCISE TREATISE OF THE VARIOUS BREEDS OF DOGS
THEIR ORIGINS AND USES. WRITTEN EXPRESSLY
FOR THE NOVICE

CONTAINING A COMPREHENSIVE MODE OF

REATMENT BOTH IN HEALTH AND SICKNESS

TOGETHER WITH THE

NAMES OF SOME PROMINENT BREEDERS

BY

H. W. HUNTINGTON
PRESIDENT OF THE NATIONAL GREYHOUND CLUB OF AMERICA

❦

ILLUSTRATED WITH HALF-TONES OF TYPICAL DOGS

ORIGINAL MARGINAL ILLUSTRATIONS BY

MR. NEVILLE CAIN, CLARENCEVILLE, L. I.

NEW YORK
PUBLISHED BY THE CAXTON PRESS
1897

Copyright, 1897, by
H. W. HUNTINGTON.

THE NEW YORK TYPE-SETTING COMPANY.

CONTENTS.

	PAGE
PREFACE	7
BULLDOG	
English	9
French	11
CHESAPEAKE BAY DOG	12
COLLIE	
Rough-coated	14
Smooth-coated	16
DALMATIAN (Coach-dog)	17
GREAT DANE	19
HOUND	
Basset	21
Beagle	23
Bloodhound	25
Dachshund	27
Deerhound	29
Foxhound (American)	31
Foxhound (English)	32
Greyhound (English)	34
Harrier	36
Greyhound (Italian)	37
Otterhound	39
Wolfhound (Irish)	41
Wolfhound (Russian)	43
MASTIFF	45
MEXICAN HAIRLESS	48
NEWFOUNDLAND	49
POINTER	51
POMERANIAN	53
POODLE	
Black, curly-coated	55
Black, corded	57
White-and-red	57
PUG	
Fawn	58
Black	59
RETRIEVER	
Black, curly-coated	60
Black, flat- or wavy-coated	62

CONTENTS

	PAGE
ST. BERNARD	
Rough-coated	64
Smooth-coated	66
SCHIPPERKE	67
SETTER	
English	69
Gordon	71
Irish	73
SHEEP-DOG (Old English or Bobtail)	75
SPANIEL	
Blenheim	90
Clumber	77
Cocker	79
Field	81
Irish Water-	83
Japanese	85
King Charles	91
Prince Charles	89
Ruby	89
Sussex	87
TERRIER	
Airedale	93
Bedlington	95
Black-and-tan	97
Boston	99
Bull	101
Clydesdale	103
Dandie Dinmont	105
Fox (Smooth-coated)	107
Fox (Wire-haired)	109
Irish	110
Maltese	112
Paisley	103
Scottish	113
Skye	115
Toy	116
Welsh	117
White English	119
Yorkshire	121
WHIPPET	123
TREATMENT OF THE DOG IN HEALTH	124
TREATMENT OF THE DOG IN SICKNESS	130
TECHNICAL TERMS	138
BREEDERS' DIRECTORY	140

PREFACE.

STONEHENGE, Shaw, and others have at various times written exhaustive treatises on the dog, its care in health and sickness; and while there is no question but that they are invaluable to the owners of large kennels, I consider that they are too complex for the novice who owns but one or two dogs. They use very largely technical terms not thoroughly understood by the layman, while certain treatments prescribed are quite impracticable except where one has a kennel-man. Besides, I think not one of the above-named writers has ever told the *novice* what to avoid in selecting a puppy or a grown dog, or what good points to insist upon. Recognizing all these facts, and recalling how I strove twenty years ago to find some work that would aid me in my search for knowledge of the dog, I have concluded to write a short treatise concerning its origin, uses, and all things pertaining to it, that will aid the reader in learning its good points, and bad ones too, the proper scale of "points" that go to make up the perfect specimen, the treatment in health and sickness, and such other data as may be of value to him. Experience as a successful breeder and owner, and having won many prizes largely through "condition," confirms me in the belief that I may perhaps be able to help a fancier in purchasing the proper kind of dog, or, if he already has one, to aid him in keeping it in health, to know its value, and how to properly show it (if he is so inclined), so that its faults may be hidden to the greatest degree, while its good points may become more pronounced.

Perfection does not exist in either man or beast, so we will strive to select that specimen which has the fewest and least noticeable faults, remembering always that in the large breeds there are ten good little ones where there is one good large one.

If this work shall have aided any lover of the dog in any direction desired, it shall have done its work. If it shall have failed, the public will surely be lenient in its criticism of

THE AUTHOR.

Beaver Brook Kennels, Danvers, Mass.
BEAVER BROOK SULTAN (formerly Rustic Sultan).

THE BULLDOG (ENGLISH).

ORIGIN. — As bull-baiting existed as far back as 1209, the bulldog *must* have then existed, but its origin is unknown.

USES. — Formerly for baiting bulls, but of late years, since this "sport" has ceased to be indulged in, it is simply kept as a watchdog and for exhibition.

* SCALE OF POINTS, ETC.

	Value.		Value.
General appearance	10	Body	5
Skull	15	Back	5
Stop	5	Tail	5
Eyes	5	Fore legs and feet	5
Ears	5	Hind legs and feet	5
Face	5	Size	5
Chops	5	Coat	5
Mouth	5		
Neck and chest	5	Total	100
Shoulders	5		

GENERAL APPEARANCE. — The general appearance of the bulldog is that of a smooth-coated, thick-set, broad, powerful, and compact dog. Head massive, large in proportion to its size; face extremely short; muzzle broad, blunt, and inclined upward. Body short and well knit; limbs stout and muscular; hind quarters very

NOTE. — An asterisk denotes that the "scale of points, etc.," given are those adopted by the Specialty Club of that particular breed; the other "scale of points, etc.," are from "Dogs of the British Isles" and Mr. Rawdon B. Lee.

high and strong, but lightly made in comparison with its heavy fore parts. The dog should convey the impression of determination, strength, and activity.

HEAD.—Very large, the larger the better; forehead flat, and skin about the head very loose, hanging in large wrinkles; frontal bones very prominent, broad, square, and high, causing a deep, wide groove between the eyes, called the stop, which should be broad and deep and extend up the middle of the forehead. Eyes set low in skull, as far from the ears as possible, round, very dark, almost black, and showing no white when looking forward. Ears set high, small and thin, "rose-ear" preferred. Face short as possible, with skin deeply wrink'ed; muzzle short, broad, turned upward, and very deep from corner of eye to corner of mouth. Nose very large, broad, and black, deeply set back, almost between the eyes; nostrils large, wide, and black, with well-defined straight line between them. Flews thick, broad, pendent, and very deep, hanging over lower jaw at sides (not in front). Teeth should show when mouth is closed; jaw broad, massive, square, and tusks wide apart; lower jaw projects in front of upper, and turns up, with six small front teeth between tusks in an even row. Teeth strong and large.

NECK.—Very deep, thick, and strong, well arched, with much loose skin at throat.

SHOULDERS.—Deep, broad, slanting, and muscular; chest wide and deep.

BACK.—Short and strong, very broad at shoulders, comparatively narrow at loins, and forming the "roach" or "wheel" back.

BODY.—Well ribbed, round, deep, with belly well tucked up.

TAIL.—Set on low, jutting out, and then turned downward, free from fringe or coarse hair, rather short than long, thick at root, but tapering to a fine point carried downward, and the dog should not be able to raise it above the back.

FORE LEGS.—Wide apart, very stout, strong, and straight; pasterns short, straight, and strong; fore feet straight; toes compact and thick; knuckles prominent and high.

HIND LEGS.—Large, muscular, longer in proportion than fore legs; hocks slightly bent; lower part of legs short.

COAT.—Fine, short, close, and smooth.

STIFLES.—Round, turned outward. On account of formation the dog walks with quick, short step, apparently skimming the ground.

COLORS (in order of merit).—If bright and pure of its sort. 1st, brindles, reds, white, with their varieties, as whole fawns, fallows, etc.; 2d, pied and mixed colors.

WEIGHT.—Fifty pounds.

G. N. Phelps's, 20 Tremont Street, Boston, Mass.
MONSIEUR BOULOT.

THE BULLDOG (FRENCH).

ORIGIN.—Nothing definite can be learned of this breed of dogs. Many exhibitors claim that it is little else than a diminutive English bulldog, bred originally in Brussels and later (about 1860) in France, with the exception that it has prick-ears and generally carries them erect, as that term indicates. Its weight should not be over 24 pounds, the lighter the better. In France the breed is fast becoming very popular among the *haut ton*, and promises to be well received here. As yet there is neither a scale of points for judging nor a club to foster the breed, so the reader will be obliged to consult the picture of Mr. G. N. Phelps's winning dog, Monsieur Boulot, in order to form a correct idea as to its outline, etc. Its exceeding intelligence is greatly in favor of its becoming a popular breed of pet dogs. The extreme difficulty attending its breeding and rearing precludes the possibility of it ever becoming common. At present even ordinary specimens are held at long prices.

Robt. Millbank's, 154 West Forty-eighth Street, New York.
PRIDE.

THE CHESAPEAKE BAY DOG.

ORIGIN.—Not known positively, but probably a cross between the two Labrador dogs that swam ashore from a sinking ship in Chesapeake Bay and the English water-spaniel.

USES.—Retrieving wild fowl from the water. There are three classes of these dogs: the otter, tawny, sedge-colored, with very short hair; the curly-haired and the straight-haired, each red brown; a white spot is not unusual.

* SCALE OF POINTS, ETC.

	Value.			Value.
Head	. 15	Coat	.	. 15
Neck	. 5	Tail	.	. 5
Shoulders	. 10	Feet	.	. 10
Chest	. 15	Legs	.	. 10
Size	. 5			
Loins	. 10		Total	. 100

THE CHESAPEAKE BAY DOG.

WEIGHT.—Dogs, 80 pounds; bitches, 65 pounds.

HEIGHT.—About 25 inches in dogs; 23 inches in bitches.

Measurements are as follows: from fore toe to top of back, 25 inches; tip of nose to base of head, 10 inches; girth of body, 33 inches; breast, 9 inches; around fore foot, 6 inches; around forearm below shoulder, 7 inches; between eyes, $2\frac{1}{4}$ inches; length of ears, 5 inches; from occiput to root of tail, 35 inches; tail, 16 inches long; around muzzle below eyes, 10 inches.

The Standard says nothing as to the dog's conformation. The illustration, therefore, must be the guide.

J. Pierpont Morgan's, New York.
RUFFORD ORMONDE.

THE COLLIE (ROUGH-COATED).

ORIGIN.—It is among the oldest of known breeds of dogs, and probably came from India. Buffon, the great writer, considers it the *parent of all dogs*.

USES.—Attending flocks of sheep and herds of cattle.

* SCALE OF POINTS, ETC.

	Value.		Value.
Head and expression	15	Tail	5
Ears	10	Coat with frill	20
Neck and shoulders	10	Size	5
Legs and feet	15		
Hind quarters	10	Total	100
Back and loins	10		

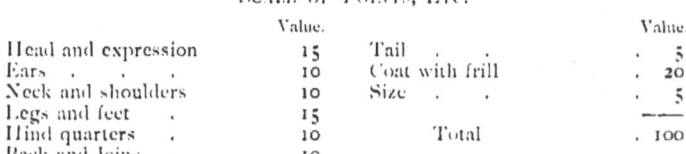

GENERAL APPEARANCE.—A lithe, active dog, presenting an elegant, pleasing outline, and exhibiting strength, speed, and intelligence.

HEAD.—Moderately long, covered with short, soft hair; skull flat, moderately wide between the ears and tapering to the eyes;

THE COLLIE (ROUGH-COATED).

very little stop; skin on head very tightly drawn; muzzle of fair length, tapering to the nose, which should always be black; mouth a bit overshot. Eyes of fair size, not prominent, placed rather wide apart, almond-shaped, and set obliquely; they may be any shade of brown, the darker the better. Ears small, covered with short, soft hair, and carried semi-erect when at attention, at other times thrown back.

NECK.—Long, arched, and muscular; chest deep and narrow in front, but wide behind the shoulders.

BACK.—Short and level; shoulders oblique; loins rather long, slightly arched, and powerful.

LEGS.—Fore legs straight and muscular, with a fair amount of flat bone; hind legs sinewy; hind quarters drooping slightly, very long from hips to hocks; stifles well bent; hip bones rather wide and ragged, and hocks well bent; pasterns long, springy, and lighter in bone than rest of leg; feet with soles well padded, and the toes arched and compact.

TAIL.—Moderately long, carried low when quiet, gaily when excited, and almost straight when running.

COAT.—An important point. It should be abundant except on head and legs; the outer coat straight, hard, and rather stiff, the inner coat soft and furry and very dense, so as to make it difficult to find the skin; the frill very abundant; hair on tail very profuse, and on hips long and bushy; fore legs slightly feathered; hind legs below hocks smooth.

COLOR.—Immaterial.

HEIGHT.—Dogs, 21 to 24 inches; bitches, 2 inches less.

WEIGHT.—Dogs, 45 to 60 pounds; bitches, 40 to 50 pounds.

DEFECTS.

Domed skull; high-peaked, occipital bone; heavy, pendulous ears; full, soft eyes; heavy, feathered legs; short tail.

J. Carver's, Newburg, N. Y.
BEN.

THE COLLIE (SMOOTH-COATED).

ORIGIN, USES, SCALE OF POINTS, etc., same as the rough collie, except in matter of coat, which should be hard, dense, and quite smooth.

J. Dickman Brown's.
PERRY.

THE DALMATIAN (COACH-DOG).

ORIGIN.—Probably indigenous to Dalmatia, a province of Austria, but records of the sixteenth century describe such a dog as belonging to Spain. The latest authentic trace is to Denmark, where it was used for drawing carts. Resembles the pointer in form.

USES.—Simply to follow the coach or equestrian.

* SCALE OF POINTS, ETC.

	Value.		Value.
Head and eyes	10	Color and markings	30
Ears	5	Tail	5
Neck and shoulders	10	Symmetry	10
Body, back, chest, and loins	10		
Legs and feet	15	Total	100
Coat	5		

GENERAL APPEARANCE.—Strong, muscular, active; free from coarseness; capable of speed and great endurance.

HEAD.—Fair length; skull flat, broad between ears; moderate stop, and *not* in straight line from occiput to nose; no wrinkles;

muzzle long and powerful; lips clean cut, fitting jaws closely. Eyes moderately wide apart, medium size, round, bright. In black-spotted dogs eyes are dark; in livers, light or light brown (yellow). Rims around eyes black in black-spotted varieties, and brown in the liver-spotted ones, *never* flesh-colored. Ears set on high, rather wide at base, tapering, carried close, thin, fine, *always* spotted. Nose black in blacks, brown in livers.

NECK AND SHOULDERS.—Neck fairly long, arched, light, tapering, *not* throaty; shoulders sloping and muscular.

BODY, BACK, CHEST, AND LOINS.—Chest very deep, not too wide; ribs well sprung, *never* rounded; powerful back; loins strong and arched.

LEGS AND FEET.—Fore legs perfectly straight, strong in bone; elbows close to body; cat-footed, tough pads; hocks well let down. Nails in black-spotted ones are black and white; in liver-spotted, brown and white.

TAIL.—Not too long, tapering well to end, carried with slight curl upward, *never* curled; the more profusely spotted, the better.

COAT.—Short, dense, hard, fine, sleek, and glossy, never woolly nor silky.

COLOR AND MARKINGS.—Ground color is *pure* unmixed white. The spots of the black-spotted variety are black, in liver-spotted variety are brown; should not intermingle, but be distinct, and about size of ten-cent silver piece on body; on head, face, ears, legs, and tail, much smaller.

WEIGHT.—Dogs, 55 pounds; bitches, 50 pounds.

G. A. Burt's, Parkersburg, W. Va.
MAJOR McKINLEY II.

THE GREAT DANE.

ORIGIN.—Probably indigenous to Germany, where it was formerly known under the various names of Ulmer, German mastiff, and boarhound.

USES.—Companion and guard for foresters and gamekeepers, also for attacking the wild boar and other beasts.

* Scale of Points, Etc.

	Value.		Value.
General appearance	3	Tail	4
Condition	3	Fore quarters	10
Activity	5	Hind quarters	10
Head	15	Feet	8
Neck	5	Coat	4
Chest	8	Size (height)	13
Back	8		
Belly	4	Total	100

General Appearance.—Large and muscular, strongly but elegantly built; movements easy and graceful; not so heavy as the mastiff, nor too much of the greyhound type.

Head.—Long, very little indentation between eyes; skull not too broad; muzzle broad, strong, and blunt; cheek muscles well developed; nose large, bridge arched; lips blunt, not hanging too much over the sides; lower jaw slightly projecting. Eyes small, round, deeply set, sharp expression. Ears small, greyhound-like, usually cropped.

Neck.—Rather long, strong and muscular, well arched, no dewlap.

Chest.—Not too broad, very deep in brisket.

Back.—Not too long; loins arched.

Stern.—Reaching to hocks, strong at root, ending fine with a slight curve; should *never* curve over the back.

Belly.—Well drawn up.

Fore Quarters.—Shoulders sloping; elbows well under, straight; legs heavy-boned, strong, and quite straight.

Hind Quarters.—Thighs muscular; hocks well let down, as in the greyhound.

Feet.—Large and round; toes well arched and close; nails very strong and curved.

Hair.—Very short, hard, and close.

Height (minimum).—Dogs, 30 inches; bitches, 28 inches.

Weight (minimum).—Dogs, 120 pounds; bitches, 100 pounds. Nothing under these should compete.

Color.—Various shades of gray, red, black, pure white, or white with patches of above colors; also brindles and mottled colors.

(From *Modern Dogs*.)

THE HOUND (BASSET).

ORIGIN.—Probably of French origin, yet closely allied to the dachshund, though larger and heavier in every particular.

USES.—Having a very keen nose, is used for the general purposes of the smaller hounds, viz., for rabbits.

* SCALE OF POINTS, ETC.

	Value.		Value.
Head, skull, eyes, muzzle, and flews	15	Stern	5
Ears	15	Coat and skin	10
Neck, dewlap, chest, and shoulders	10	Color and markings	15
Fore legs and feet	15	Character and symmetry	5
Back, loins, and hind quarters	10	Total	100

HEAD.—Closely resembling the bloodhound's; long, narrow, heavy flews; occiput prominent; forehead wrinkled to the eyes, which should be kind and show the haw. Teeth small, and the

protruding of the upper jaw is *not* a fault. Ears so long that in hunting the dog treads on them, set low, hang loose in folds, ends curl inward, thin and velvety.

NECK.—Powerful, with heavy dewlaps; elbows *must not* turn out; chest deep and full; body long and low.

LEGS AND FEET.—Fore legs short (about 4 inches), close-fitting to chest; massive paw, each toe standing out distinctly.

STIFLES.—Well bent; quarters muscular, giving the dog a barrel-like shape and a peculiar waddling gait.

STERN.—Coarse underneath, and carried hound fashion, i.e., carried gaily.

COAT.—Short, smooth, fine, and glossy; skin loose and elastic.

COLOR.—Black, white and tan, with black patches on back; also *sometimes* hare-pied.

WEIGHT.—Thirty to forty-five pounds.

H. L. Kreuder's, Nanuet, N. Y.
FRANK FOREST.

THE HOUND (BEAGLE).

ORIGIN.—This breed seems to be little else than a diminutive foxhound; has long been in existence; probably one of the oldest of British dogs.

USES.—Hunting rabbits, and generally run in packs of five to ten couples; they are merry little fellows, sturdy and gamy, with a most musical tongue and a very keen nose.

* SCALE OF POINTS, ETC.

	Value.		Value.
Skull	5	Ribs	5
Ears	15	Fore legs and feet	10
Eyes	10	Hips, thighs, and hind legs	10
Muzzle, jaw, and lips	5	Tail	5
Neck	5	Coat	5
Shoulders and chest	10		
Back and loins	15	Total	100

HEAD.—Skull moderately domed. Ears set on low, long and fine in leather, rather broad and rounded at tips, absence of all erectile power. Eyes full, prominent, rather wide apart, soft and lustrous. Muzzle medium length, squarely cut; stop well defined; jaws level; lips either free from or with moderate flews; nostrils large.

NECK AND THROAT.—Neck free in action, strong, yet not loaded; throat clean, free from folds of skin.

SHOULDERS AND CHEST.—Shoulders somewhat sloping, muscular, but not loaded; chest moderately broad and full.

BACK, LOINS, AND RIBS.—Back short and strong; loins broad and slightly arched; ribs well sprung.

FORE LEGS AND FEET.—Fore legs straight, plenty of bone; feet close, firm, either round or hare-like.

HIPS, THIGHS, AND HIND LEGS.—Hips muscular; stifles strong and well let down; hocks firm.

TAIL.—Carried gaily, well up, medium curve, and clothed with a decided brush.

HEIGHT.—Fifteen inches.

COLOR.—All hound colors admissible. (See Foxhound.)

DEFECTS.

Flat skull; short ears, set on too high, pointed at tips; eyes yellow or light color; muzzle snipy; thick, short neck; elbows out; knees knuckled over; long tail with "tea-pot" curve.

DISQUALIFICATIONS.

Eyes close together and terrier-like; thin rat-tail, with absence of brush; short, nappy coat.

J. L. Winchell's, Fair Haven, Vt.
CHAMPION VICTOR.

THE HOUND (BLOODHOUND).

ORIGIN.—In Barbour's "Bruce" (1489) we find the earliest mention of the bloodhound, where it is called the "sleuthhund." However, little can be learned definitely of its origin.

USES.—Having scenting powers to a marvelous degree, it is used in trailing wounded deer, slaves, sheep-stealers, escaped convicts, etc.

DISPOSITION.—Contrary to general impressions, the modern bloodhound is of a most equable disposition, kind and gentle, and quite apt to be timid, excepting when on the trail; then it is extremely dangerous.

SCALE OF POINTS, ETC.

	Value.		Value.
Head	15	Legs and feet	20
Ears and eyes	10	Color and coat	10
Flews	5	Stern	5
Neck	5	Symmetry	10
Shoulders and chest	10		
Back and ribs	10	Total	100

HEAD.—This is the most distinguishable feature of the dog; it is domed, blunt at occiput; jaws very long and wide at nostrils, hollow and very lean at cheek; brows very prominent, and the general expression is grand and majestic; skin covering cheeks and forehead wrinkled to a wonderful degree.

EYES AND EARS.—Eyes hazel, rather small, deeply sunk, showing haw, which is deep red. This redness, some claim, is indicative of cross with mastiff, Gordon setter, or St. Bernard. Ears long, and will overlap when drawn over front of nose, hang close to cheek, *never* inclined to be pricked; leather thin, covered with soft hair.

FLEWS.—Very long and pendent, falling below mouth.

NECK.—Long, so as to enable the dog to easily drop his nose to the ground; considerable dewlap.

CHEST AND SHOULDERS.—Chest wider than deep; shoulders sloping and muscular.

BACK AND BACK RIBS.—Wide and deep, the hips being wide or almost ragged.

LEGS AND FEET.—Legs *must* be straight and muscular; feet as cat-like as possible.

COAT.—Short and hard on body, silky on ears and top of head.

COLOR.—Black and tan or tan only; the black extends to the back, sides, top of neck, and top of head; the tan should be of deep, rich red; there should be little or no white.

STERN.—Carried gaily in gentle curve, but not raised above back; lower side is fringed with hair.

DEFECT.

Absence of black.

J. H. Snow's, Philadelphia, Pa.
FRITZ.

THE HOUND (DACHSHUND).

ORIGIN.—The origin of this dog is lost in antiquity. A dog resembling it very closely is to be found on the monument of Thothmes III., 2000 B.C. The modern dog is essentially German.

USES.—Hunting rabbits and hares, tracking wounded animals and badgers.

* SCALE OF POINTS, ETC.

	Value.		Value.
Head and skull	12	Chest	7
Jaw	5	Skin and coat	13
Legs and feet	20	Stern	5
Loins	8	Color	4
Body	$8\frac{1}{2}$		
Symmetry and quality	11	Total	100
Ears	$6\frac{1}{2}$		

HEAD AND SKULL.—Long, level, narrow; peak well developed; no stop. Eyes intelligent and rather small; follow body in color. Ears long, broad, soft, set on low and well back, carried close to head. Jaws strong, level, square to the muzzle; canines recurvant.

CHEST.— Deep, narrow; breast-bone prominent.

LEGS AND FEET.— Fore legs very short, strong in bone, well crooked, not standing over; elbows well muscled, neither in nor out; feet large, round, strong, with thick pads and strong nails. Hind legs smaller in bone and higher; feet smaller. The dog must stand equally on all parts of the foot.

SKIN AND COAT.— Skin thick, loose, supple, and in great quantity; coat dense, short, and strong.

LOINS.— Well arched, long, and muscular.

STERN.— Long and strong, flat at root, tapering to tip; hair on under side coarse; carried low except when excited.

BODY.— Length from back of head to root of tail two and a half times height at shoulder; fore ribs well sprung; back ribs very short.

COLOR.— Any color; nose to follow body color; *much* white objectionable.

SYMMETRY AND QUALITY.— The dachshund should be long, low, and graceful, not cloddy.

WEIGHT.— Dogs, 21 pounds; bitches, 18 pounds.

Albion L. Page's, 69 Wall Street, New York.
LOCHIEL.

THE HOUND (DEERHOUND).

ORIGIN.—Undoubtedly descended from the Irish wolfhound, though some claim it to be either a cross of foxhound and greyhound, or greyhound and bloodhound. It is first mentioned in 1528 as a distinct breed.

USES.—Hunting deer.

SCALE OF POINTS, ETC.

	Value.		Value.
Head and skull	15	Coat	8
Eyes and ears	10	Stern	5
Neck and chest	10	Color	5
Body	10	Symmetry	15
Thighs and hocks	12		
Legs and feet	10	Total	100

HEAD.—Skull resembles that of a coarse, large greyhound, long and wide between ears; stop very slight. Jaws long; teeth level and strong; nostrils open, but not very wide; cheeks muscular; bone under eye neither prominent nor hollow. Ears small, thin, carried a trifle higher than those of the greyhound, but should turn over at tips; pricked ears very objectionable; they should be thinly fringed with hair at edges only. Eyes full, and dark hazel, sometimes blue.

NECK.—Long enough to allow the dog to stoop to the scent at a fast pace.

CHEST AND SHOULDERS.—Chest deep rather than wide, resembling that of greyhound; girth of a full-size dog deerhound should be at least 2 inches greater than its height; shoulders long, oblique, and muscular.

BACK AND BACK RIBS.—Back should be powerful; a good loin should measure 25 or 26 inches; back ribs are often rather shallow, but they should be well sprung; loins arched, drooping to root of tail.

ELBOWS AND STIFLES.—Elbows well let down to give length to true arm, and quite straight; stifles wide apart, well bent.

SYMMETRY is essential to its position as a companionable dog.

QUALITY is also to be regarded as of great importance.

LEGS AND QUARTERS.—Great bone and muscle are essential; the bones must be well put together at knees and hocks, which should be long and well developed; quarters deep, but seldom wide, with considerable slope to tail.

FEET.—Well arched and cat-like.

COLOR AND COAT.—The colors are dark blue, fawn, grizzle, and brindle, the latter with more or less tint of blue; the fawn should have tips of ears dark; the grizzle generally has a decided tint of blue; white on breast or toes should not disqualify a dog. Coat is coarser on back than elsewhere, and many claim it should be intermediate between silk and wool, and not the coarse hair often met with. The whole body is clothed with a rough coat, sometimes amounting to shagginess; that of muzzle is longer in proportion than elsewhere, but the mustache should not be wiry, and should stand out in irregular tufts; there should be no approach to feather on legs, but their inside should be hairy.

TAIL.—Long and gently curved, without any twist, thinly clothed with hair only.

F. J. Hagan's, Louisville, Ky.
BIG STRIVE.

THE HOUND (AMERICAN FOXHOUND).

ORIGIN.—A breed of dogs descended from the English species, but bred on lighter and finer lines. For uses and scale of points, see English Foxhound.

McGregor & Bragdon's, Portsmouth, N. H.
SONGSTER.

THE HOUND (ENGLISH FOXHOUND).

ORIGIN.—A breed probably indigenous to Great Britain, and quite ancient too. Its absolute origin is unknown.

USES.—Hunting foxes and deer (giving tongue when in full chase); also in America for hounding deer, moose, and other large game.

* SCALE OF POINTS, ETC.

	Value.		Value.
Head	15	Legs and feet	20
Neck	5	Color and coat	5
Shoulders	10	Stern	5
Chest and back ribs	10	Symmetry	5
Back and loins	10		
Hind quarters	10	Total	100
Elbows	5		

HEAD.—Full size, but not heavy; brow pronounced, but not high; of good length, so girth will be 16 inches. Nose long and wide. Ears low set on and lying close to cheeks.

NECK.—Long and clean, without throatiness.

THE HOUND (ENGLISH FOXHOUND).

SHOULDERS.—Long, well muscled, sloping, and the true arm long and muscular.

CHEST AND BACK RIBS.—Girth of chest over 30 inches in 24-inch-tall hound; back ribs very deep.

BACK AND LOINS.—Very muscular; couplings wide even to raggedness, with slight arch of loins.

HIND QUARTERS.—Very strong, as great endurance is required; elbows set straight, neither in nor out.

LEGS AND FEET.—Legs as straight as gun-barrels and as strong; large size of bone at ankle all-important; feet round, cat-like, and strong.

COLOR AND COAT.—Color black tan and white, black and white, and various pies of white and the color of the hare and badger; coat dense, short, hard, and glossy.

STERN.—Generally arched, carried gaily over back, fringed with hair, and tapering to a point.

SYMMETRY considerable, and quality should be evident.

Woodhaven Kennels, Woodhaven, L. I.
CHAMPION SPINAWAY.

THE HOUND (ENGLISH GREYHOUND).

ORIGIN.—Beyond question the oldest breed of dogs known, as on the pyramids of Egypt, obelisks, and ancient carved columns it is found in bold relief, with the same outlines as shown in the above illustration. In its native state it is quite devoid of courage, so the bitches are bred to bulldogs, and that product, showing most greyhound form and bulldog character, is then bred to a greyhound dog, continuing this same last breeding until in the fifth generation we produce the dog of the present day, which has indomitable courage, wonderful speed and endurance, and is possessed of a desire to kill. The name "greyhound" is a corruption of "gazehound," signifying that the dog hunts its quarry by sight and not by scent. In England and Italy none but the nobility were formerly allowed to own a greyhound, and the killing of one was then considered a felony.

USES.—Coursing hares and rabbits, and in addition, in our Western States, for killing foxes, coyotes, and wolves, though it is rarely able single-handed to kill the latter, on account of their size and ferocity.

THE HOUND (ENGLISH GREYHOUND).

Scale of Points, Etc.

	Value.		Value.
Head and eyes	10	Feet	15
Neck	10	Coat	5
Chest and fore quarters	20	Tail	5
Loins and back ribs	15		
Hind quarters	20	Total	100

HEAD.—Long and narrow, fairly large between the ears, well filled out before the eyes, little or no stop, jaws lean, and eyes bright and tolerably full. Ears small and folding down when at rest, but raised when animated. Teeth *must* be strong, and mouth *level*.

NECK.—A trifle arched, and sufficiently long to enable the dog to easily pick up a hare when in full stride.

SHOULDERS.—Placed as obliquely as possible.

CHEST.—Fairly deep, and sufficiently wide to give free action to the heart and lungs.

FORE LEGS.—*Straight*, of good bone, and length from elbow to knee twice that from knee to ground.

FEET.—The cat-foot is considered best.

LOINS.—Strong, but not too broad; back powerful and somewhat arched.

HIND QUARTERS.—Very muscular; stifles strong and well bent; hocks well let down.

TAIL.—Rat-like, fine, long, and somewhat curved, and with little hair on it.

COLOR.—Greyhounds are of any color, parti or solid.

DISPOSITION.—Kind and amiable, rarely otherwise.

WEIGHT.—Dogs, 60 pounds; bitches, 50 pounds.

Objectionable Features.

Yellow or white eyes; prick-ears; dish-face; long, separated toes; lightness of bone; weak back; straight stifles; undershot or overshot.

(From *Modern Dogs*.)

THE HOUND (HARRIER).

ORIGIN.—Is little else than a small-sized English foxhound. By some considered to be cross of "Southern hound" and beagle.

USES.—Hunting the hare, sometimes foxes and deer.

SCALE OF POINTS, ETC.

	Value.		Value.
Head	10	Legs and feet	20
Neck	5	Color and coat	5
Shoulders	10	Stern	5
Chest and back ribs	10	Symmetry	5
Back and loins	10		
Hind quarters	15	Total	100
Elbows	5		

The points are same as those of the English foxhound, except that the head is wider and heavier, nose longer and broader, ears set farther backward, not rounded.

HEIGHT.—Sixteen to twenty inches.

Frank H. Hoyt, Sharon, Pa.
TRIXIE.

THE HOUND (ITALIAN GREYHOUND).

ORIGIN.—Little is known of the origin of this breed beyond the fact that Italy and the south of France are supposed to be where it originated.

USES.—A purely pet dog, exceedingly delicate and fragile.

SCALE OF POINTS, ETC.

	Value.		Value.
Head	15	Color	10
Neck, ears, and eyes	15	Symmetry	20
Legs, feet, and fore quarters	10	Size	10
Hind quarters	10		
Tail and coat	10	Total	100

HEAD.—If possible should be like the English greyhound's, but such formation is now rarely met with. In all recent exhibits the skull is more or less round, and face, though still pointed, is too short, with tendency to turn up.

NECK.—Long and elegant, resembling closely its larger congener.

EARS AND EYES.—Ears an exact counterpart of the English greyhound's, though always somewhat enlarged in comparison with body. Eyes much larger proportionately, soft and languishing, but should never weep; color of iris is usually a dark brown.

LEGS, FEET, AND FORE QUARTERS.—Same as the greyhound's.

HIND QUARTERS.—As with the last two paragraphs, the only difference lies in comparative value, the English dog's points being estimated from the workmanlike view, while the Italian is regarded from an artistic standpoint.

TAIL.—Somewhat shorter than the English dog's, but it *must* be gently curved in same tobacco-pipe way, fine in bone, except at root, as well as free from hair.

COAT.—Short, soft, and silky.

COLOR.—Largely to be taken into consideration, and is consequently estimated at a high figure. Fawns are now far in the ascendant, and to no other color should the *full* value be accorded. A small star on breast or white toe takes off a point or two, according to extent of white, but in *all* cases toe-nails should be dark.

SYMMETRY.—Must be carefully estimated, as a want of elegance in detail or of combination in due proportion alike lowers the value of these points separately to a very low ebb. It is a high-stepping little aristocrat.

SIZE.—Bitch for modern successful exhibition should be little over 5 pounds, *nor should the dog exceed* 7 *or* 7½ *pounds.*

(From *Modern Dogs*.)

THE HOUND (OTTERHOUND).

ORIGIN.—Nothing positive is known about it, but probably a cross of Welsh harrier, "Southern hound," and a terrier, though some say it is of bloodhound extraction. The breed is very old.

USES.—For hunting the otter and other water-animals.

SCALE OF POINTS, ETC.

	Value.		Value.
Skull	10	Legs and feet	10
Jaws	10	Coat	10
Eyes	5	Stern	5
Ears	10	Symmetry and strength	10
Chest and shoulders	15		
Body and loins	15	Total	100

GENERAL APPEARANCE.—Always excepting coat, it much resembles the bloodhound; it should be perfect in symmetry, strongly built, hard and enduring, with unfailing powers of scent and a natural antipathy to the game it is bred to pursue.

HEAD.—Large, broader in proportion than the bloodhound's; forehead high; muzzle a fair length, and nostrils wide. Ears long, thin, and pendulous, fringed with hair.

NECK.—Not naturally long, and looks shorter than it really is from the abundance of hair on it.

SHOULDERS.—Slope well.

LEGS AND FEET.—Legs straight, and feet a good size; compact.

BACK.—Strong and wide; ribs, and particularly the back ribs, well let down.

THIGHS.—Big and firm, and hocks well let down.

STERN.—Well and thickly covered with hair, and carried well up, but not curled.

COLORS are generally grizzle or sandy, with black and tan more or less clearly defined.

(From *Modern Dogs*.)

THE HOUND (IRISH WOLFHOUND).

ORIGIN.—Lost in antiquity; considered by some to be the parent of the deerhound. Good specimens are rarely to be met with these days.

USES.—Hunting wolves, and frequently deer.

* Description from Mr. Rawdon B. Lee's "Modern Dogs" (Sporting).

GENERAL APPEARANCE.—Not so heavy or massive as the Great Dane, but more so than the deerhound, which in general type it should otherwise resemble. Of great size and commanding appearance; very muscular; strongly, though gracefully, built; movements easy and active; head and neck carried high; tail carried with upward sweep, with a slight curve toward the extremity.

HEAD.—Long; frontal bones of forehead very slightly raised, and very little indentation between eyes; skull not too broad; muzzle long and moderately pointed. Ears small and greyhound-like in carriage.

NECK.—Rather long, very strong and muscular, well arched, without dewlap or loose skin about throat.

CHEST.—Very deep; breast wide.

BACK.—Rather long than short; loins arched.

TAIL.—Long, slightly curved, moderate thickness, well covered with hair.

BELLY.—Well drawn up.

FORE QUARTERS.—Shoulders muscular, giving breadth of chest, set sloping; elbows well under, neither turned inward nor outward; forearm muscular; the whole leg strong and quite straight.

HIND QUARTERS.—Muscular thighs, and second thigh long and strong, as in greyhound; hocks well let down, turned neither in nor out.

FEET.—Moderately large and round, neither turned inward nor outward; toes well arched and closed; nails very strong, and curved.

HAIR.—Rough and hard on body, legs, and head; especially wiry and long over eyes and under jaw.

COLOR AND MARKINGS.—The colors are gray, brindle, red, black, pure white, fawn, or any color that appears in the deerhound.

HEIGHT AND WEIGHT.—Minimum height and weight of dogs is 31 inches and 120 pounds; of bitches, 28 inches and 90 pounds. Anything below this should be debarred from competition. Great size is the desideratum to be aimed at.

DEFECTS.

Too light or heavy a head; too highly arched frontal bone; large ears, and hanging flat to face; short neck; full dewlap; too narrow or too broad a chest; sunken, or hollow, or quite straight back; bent fore legs, overbent fetlocks, twisted feet, spreading toes; too curly a tail; weak hind quarters and a general want of muscle; too short in body.

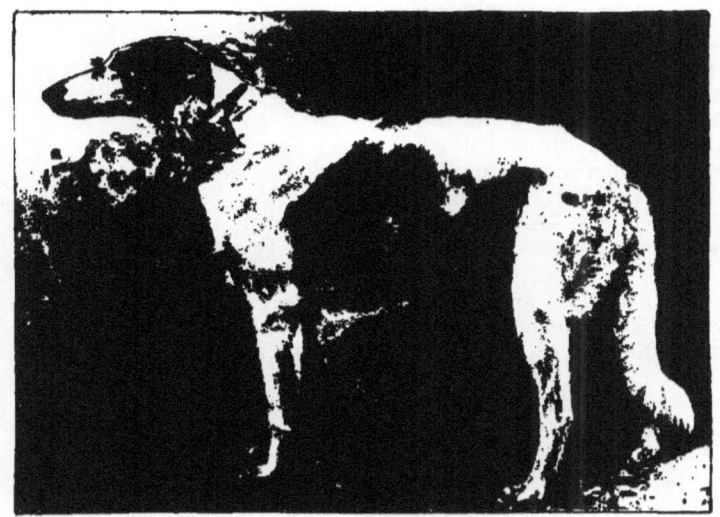

George M. Keasbey's, Newark, N. J.
OPTIMIST.

THE HOUND (RUSSIAN WOLFHOUND).

ORIGIN.—The Russians do not seem to have an exact or even a clear idea as to the origin of this breed. It in all probability came from Persia, as it is more like the dog of that nation than it is like the deerhound. It is of the greyhound family, however.

USES.—Attacking wolves and foxes, though it can rarely single-handed kill the former.

* SCALE OF POINTS, ETC.

	Value.		Value.
Head and muzzle .	15	Legs and feet .	10
Eyes and ears .	10	Stern . . .	5
Neck and chest .	10	Coat . . .	5
Back and loins .	15	General symmetry	15
Ribs . . .	5		
Thighs and hocks	10	Total	100

HEAD.—Generally very long, and lean throughout; flat, narrow skull; stop hardly perceptible; long snout. Nose black, and frequently Roman. Eyes dark, expressive, oblong. Ears small; thin leather; set on high; tips almost touching when thrown back.

NECK.—Not too short, nor rising straight.

SHOULDERS.—Clean and sloping.

CHEST.—Somewhat narrow, but not hollow.

BACK.—Rather bony, and free from any hollow; well arched in male, but level and broad in female; loins broad and drooping; ribs deep, not so well sprung as in the greyhound, reaching to elbow.

FORE LEGS.—Lean and straight.

HIND LEGS.—Somewhat under body when standing still; not straight; stifles only slightly bent; legs not too far apart; pasterns short.

FEET.—Long toes, closely joined; nails short and strong; feet covered with fur like a hare.

COAT.—Long, soft, silky.

TAIL.—Long and sickle-shaped.

COLOR.—Any color.

HEIGHT AND WEIGHT.—Height for a dog, from 28 to 31 inches at shoulder; bitch, about 2 inches less. The male should be shorter in body than the female. Weight: dog, 75 to 100 pounds; bitch, 60 to 75 pounds.

CHAMPION BEAUFORT'S BLACK PRINCE.

THE MASTIFF.

ORIGIN.—Its origin is purely conjectural. It certainly is a dog of the British Isles, as at the time of Cæsar it was in existence there.

USES.—A grand, awe-inspiring dog; an excellent guardian, courageous and most companionable.

* SCALE OF POINTS, ETC.

	Value.		Value.
Shape of skull	10	Thighs	3
Girth of skull	10	Stern	3
Ears—carriage and size	5	Legs	3
Muzzle—bluntness, breadth, depth, lips, color (each 3 points)	15	Feet	2
		Size, height, and general appearance of bulk	15
Neck	4	Coat	5
Breadth of breast	4	Fawns, dark ears and muzzle, or brindle with dark ears and muzzle	5
Loins and back	4		
Girth of chest	4		
Shoulders	4		
Length	4	Total	100

GENERAL CHARACTER.—Large, massive, powerful, symmetrical, and well knit; a combination of grandeur and good nature, courage and docility.

HEAD.—Square when viewed from any point; breadth greatly to be desired, and should be in ratio to length of the whole head and face as 2 to 3.

BODY.—Massive, broad, deep, long, powerfully built; legs wide apart, squarely set; muscles sharply defined; size a great desideratum if combined with quality; height of less importance than substance.

SKULL.—Broad between ears; forehead flat, wrinkled; muscles of temples and cheeks well developed; arch across skull a rounded, flattened curve, and a depression up center of forehead.

FACE OR MUZZLE.—Short, broad under eyes, keeping nearly parallel in width to end of nose; blunt, cut off square, thus forming a right angle with upper line of face, of great depth from point of nose to under jaw; under jaw broad to end. Teeth powerful, wide apart, incisors level, or the lower projecting beyond the upper, but never sufficiently so as to become visible when mouth is closed. Length of muzzle to whole head and face as 1 to 3; circumference of muzzle (between eyes and nose) to that of head (before the ears) as 3 to 5. Ears small, thin, wide apart, set on high, flat, and close to cheeks when in repose. Eyes small, wide apart, divided by at least the space of two eyes; stop well marked, but not too abrupt; color hazel brown, the darker the better, showing no haw. Nose broad, with widely spreading nostrils; flat (not pointed nor turned up). Lips slightly pendulous.

NECK.—Slightly arched, moderately long, very muscular.

CHEST.—Wide, deep, well let down; ribs arched and well rounded; false ribs deep and well set back to hips.

SHOULDER AND ARM.—Slightly sloping, heavy and muscular.

FORE LEGS AND FEET.—Straight, strong, set wide apart; bones very large; elbows square; pasterns upright. Feet large and round; toes well arched up; nails black.

BACK, LOINS, AND FLANKS.—Wide and muscular; flat and very wide in a bitch, slightly arched in a dog.

HIND QUARTERS AND THIGHS.—Broad, wide, muscular; well-developed second thighs; stifles straight; hocks bent, wide apart, and squarely set when standing or walking; feet round and *without* dew-claws.

TAIL.—Put on high up, reaching to hocks, or a little below; wide at root, tapering; hanging straight in repose, but forming a curve with end pointing upward, but not over the back, when the dog is excited.

COAT.—Short and close-lying, not too fine over shoulders, neck, and back.

COLOR.—Apricot or silver fawn, or dark fawn-brindle; muzzle, ears, and nose should be black, with black round the orbits and extending upward between them. Fawns and brindles without dark points, reds without black muzzle, and pies, award no points for color.

WEIGHT.—Dogs 27 inches should weigh 120 pounds.

Mrs. H. T. Foote's, New Rochelle, N. Y.
ME TOO.

THE MEXICAN HAIRLESS.

ORIGIN.—One of the oldest of known breeds, being found nearly all over the world, but best known as coming from Mexico, where its origin is unknown.

USES.—A pet dog.

DESCRIPTION.—A smart-looking sort of terrier of some kind, with perhaps a bit of greyhound blood in it. There is no scale of points, nor is there any club organized to foster the breed. It is entirely devoid of hair, except sometimes a tuft or crest on its head and a few straggling hairs on various parts of the body. It is a lively little fellow, mostly of a brown color, and, though devoid of hair, can stand the cold very well. It has a rounded body, a bit cobby in appearance, with somewhat of a terrier head. Weight is about 15 pounds.

BOODLES, ESQ.

THE NEWFOUNDLAND.

ORIGIN.—Indigenous to Newfoundland, from which it takes its name. This dog is probably a cross of some of the European dogs, some writers claiming that it shows the blood of both the St. Bernard and the water-spaniel.

USES.—A good companion, and a water-dog as well.

* No Scale of Points adopted.

HEAD.—Broad, massive, flat on skull; occipital bone well developed; no decided stop. Muzzle short, clean cut, and rather square in shape.

COAT.—Flat, dense, of coarsish texture, oily.

BODY.—Well ribbed up; broad back; neck strong, and muscular loins.

FORE LEGS.—Straight, muscular; elbows well let down, and feather all over.

HIND QUARTERS AND LEGS.—Hind quarters very strong; free

action of legs, which should have little feather. Dew-claws should be removed.

CHEST.—Deep, fairly broad, well covered with hair, but no frill.

BONE.—Massive, but not giving a heavy appearance.

FEET.—Large; splayed or turned-out feet objectionable.

TAIL.—Moderate length (to hocks); well covered with long hair, but no flag; in repose it should hang downward with a curve at end. Tails with kinks in them or carried over the back are objectionable.

EARS.—Small, set well back, square with the skull, close to head, and covered with short hair; no fringe.

EYES.—Small, dark brown, deeply set, but showing no haw; wide apart.

COLOR.—Jet black; a tinge of bronze or splash of white on chest and toes *not* objectionable.

HEIGHT AND WEIGHT.—Average height is 27 inches for dog, and 25 inches for bitch; weight, 100 and 85 pounds respectively.

DEFECTS.

Slack loins and cow-hocked.

Westminster Kennel Club, Babylon, L. I.
KING OF KENT.

THE POINTER.

ORIGIN.—The dog originally came from Spain, was imported into Great Britain, and undergoing many changes, no doubt by crossing with the foxhound, is to-day a vast improvement on the parent stock.

USES.—Hunting all kinds of game-birds.

SCALE OF POINTS, ETC.

	Value.		Value.
Skull	10	Feet	8
Nose	10	Tail	5
Ears, eyes, and lips	4	Coat	3
Neck	6	Color	5
Shoulders and chest	15	Symmetry and quality	7
Hind quarters and stifles	15		
Legs, elbows, and hocks	12	Total	100

Brains, nose, and speed make the pointer. The countenance should be lively and intelligent.

HEAD.—Large, flat; stop well defined, and with a depression

running from stop to occiput. The head should not be heavy, as this indicates coarseness and an unreliable disposition. A full development of occipital bone is indispensable. Nose large, long, broad (black in all except lemons and whites, when it should be deep flesh color), deep enough to make it "square"-muzzled; nostrils large and open. Ears moderately long, filbert-shaped, and lying flat; set low; leather thin and flexible; coverings silky. Eyes medium size, not set wide apart, and of the various shades of brown, varying with color of coat. Lips full; not thick nor pendulous.

NECK.—Arched, round, firm, and not too short; *no tendency* to throatiness; *no* dewlap.

SHOULDERS.—Long, sloping, and powerful.

CHEST.—Deep, with narrow sternum, sloping backward to a well-tucked-up abdomen; ribs moderately sprung, *not flat*.

HIND QUARTERS.—Loins should be broad and slightly arched; hips thick, strong, and muscular; stifles are generally straight, but should be well bent.

LEGS.—Good legs are most essential; front legs should be straight and strong, hind legs well crooked, and both should be covered with strong, compact muscles, well developed; the elbow- and hock-joints should be hinged long and set straight with sides of body.

FEET.—With surface enough to sustain the weight, but not too large; round and cat-like; pads full and tough; nails short and thick, with plenty of hair between toes.

TAIL.—Set on well up, and should taper to a decided point; the straighter it is, the better. It should be carried low, and the action should be free.

COAT.—Fairly dense, and not too soft.

COLOR.—Liver and white, black and white, orange and white, whole black, or whole liver, this being the order of preference.

NORMAN. NELLIE.

THE POMERANIAN.

ORIGIN.—Pomerania, on the Baltic Sea, is probably its home; it may, however, have come from the arctic regions, as it closely resembles the Samoyeds and Eskimo dogs.

USES.—A pet dog.

* SCALE OF POINTS.

	Value.		Value.
Head	10	Feet	10
Muzzle	5	Coat	15
Ears and eyes	5	Color	15
Shoulders	5	Tail	5
Chest	5	Symmetry	5
Loins	10		
Legs	10	Total	100

HEAD.—Resembles greatly that of collie, being even more tapering and fox-like; a slight furrow down middle of forehead, and more brow than in that dog; very prominent occiput; muzzle collie-like; nose black at tip, even in perfectly white specimens; also a slight tendency in upper teeth to be overshot.

EARS AND EYES.—Ears perfectly pricked, small, and neat in shape. Eyes large, dark brown, and set obliquely, close together.

SHOULDERS.—Oblique.

CHEST.—Generally round, with back ribs shallow.

LOINS.—Frequently defective from shallow back ribs.

LEGS.—Straight, muscular, with elbows well let down; good, strong stifles; clean hocks.

FEET.—Small, round, cat-like; thin, and unfit for road-work.

COAT.—Like very coarse fur, with under coat furry also; face is bare of hair.

COLOR.—Jet black without white; pure white is allowable, also red.

TAIL.—Carried over back on one side (left); heavily feathered.

SYMMETRY.—Of the spitz style.

WEIGHT.—Limit, 20 pounds; 7 pounds preferred.

H. G. Trevor's, Southampton, L. I.
CHAMPION MILO.

THE POODLE (BLACK, CURLY-COATED).

ORIGIN.—There is little doubt but that the poodle of to-day finds its origin in the old "water-dog" of France, where it was not only used for retrieving wounded water-fowl, but for swimming-contests, when the hind parts were clipped or shaven in order to give freer action to the legs.

USES.—A very bright, intelligent companion, and a good retriever.

* SCALE OF POINTS, ETC.

	Value.		Value.
Head, muzzle, and eyes	20	Coat	20
Neck and chest	5	Color	10
Back and loins	10	Symmetry	15
Legs and feet	15		
Stern	5	Total	100

GENERAL APPEARANCE.—Strong, active, intelligent, cobby in build, and perfectly coated with close curls or long "cords."

HEAD.—Long; skull large, wide between the eyes, slight peak; parts over eyes well arched; the whole covered with curls or cords. Muzzle long (not snipy), slightly tapering, not too deep; stop well defined. Teeth level and strong; black roof of mouth preferable. Eyes medium size, dark, bright, and set at right angles with the line of face. Nose large, perfectly black; wide-open nostrils. Ears very long, close to cheek, low set, and well covered with ringlets or curls.

NECK.—Very strong, admitting head to be carried high.

CHEST.—Fairly deep, but not too wide, well covered with muscles.

LEGS.—Fore legs perfectly straight, and not so long as to be leggy; hind legs muscular, well bent, with hocks low down.

FEET.—Strong, slightly spread, standing well on toes; nails black; pads large and hard.

BACK.—Fair length; well-ribbed-up body; loins strong and muscular.

TAIL.—Carried at angle of 45 degrees, with long ringlets or cords. Preferable length, 3 to 5 inches.

COAT.—If corded, cords should be thick and strong, hanging in long, ropy cords. If curly, the curls close, thick, and of silky texture.

WEIGHT.—From 40 to 60 pounds.

Only three colors are admitted, black, white, and red, and they should be without mixture.

W. Grebe's, 1398 Second Avenue, New York.
TELL.

THE POODLE (BLACK, CORDED).

For origin, uses, scale of points, etc., see The Poodle (Black, Curly-coated).

THE POODLE (WHITE-AND-RED).

* SCALE OF POINTS, ETC.

Same as the black poodle, *except:*

EYES.—Yellow or light blue, free from black rims around eyelids.
NOSE.—Red or liver color.
NAILS.—Red or pink.
BACK.—Spots on back should be red or liver, and the entire body free from black ticks.

Rookery Kennels, Painesville, O.
HAUGHTY MADGE.

THE PUG (FAWN).

ORIGIN.—It is generally conceded that this breed is a cross between the fawn-colored, smooth English terrier and the jet-black Chinese terrier. Vero Shaw *et al.* concede this point.

USES.—Purely a pet dog, with a fair amount of intelligence.

* SCALE OF POINTS, ETC.

	Value.		Value.
Symmetry	10	Mask	5
Size	5	Wrinkles	5
Condition	5	Tail	5
Body	10	Trace	5
Legs and feet	10	Coat	5
Head	5	Color	5
Muzzle	5	Carriage	5
Ears	5		
Eyes	10	Total	100

GENERAL APPEARANCE.—Square and cobby.

SIZE AND CONDITION.—The weight is from 12 to 15 pounds, and the dog should be shown with bones well covered and muscles well developed.

BODY.—Short and cobby; chest wide; ribs well sprung.
LEGS.—Strong, straight, of moderate length, and well under body.
FEET.—Between style of cat- and harefoot, well-split-up toes, and *black nails*.
MUZZLE.—Short, square, blunt, but not upturned.
HEAD.—Large, round, *not apple-headed*, with *no* indentation of the skull. Eyes dark, very large, bold and prominent, soft and solicitous in expression, lustrous, and when excited full of fire. Ears thin, small, and soft. The button-ear is preferred to the rose-ear.
MARKINGS.—Clearly defined: the muzzle or mask, ears, moles on cheeks, thumb-marks or diamond on forehead, and back trace should be as black as possible.
MASK.—Black; the more defined, the better.
WRINKLES.—Deep and large.
TAIL.—Curled lightly as possible over hip. The double curl is perfection.
COAT.—Fine, smooth, soft, short, glossy, *neither hard nor woolly*.
COLOR.—Silver or apricot fawn. Each should be very decided, so as to make a contrast between color and trace.

DEFECTS.

Long-legged or short-legged.

THE PUG (BLACK).

ORIGIN.—Beyond question a dog of Chinese origin, as Lady Brassey brought several specimens from there to London, and other travelers have seen them there.
USES.—A pet dog only.

* SCALE OF POINTS, ETC.

Same in all respects as for the fawn pug, excepting that the coat should be pure black and entirely free from white.

(From *Modern Dogs*)

THE RETRIEVER (BLACK, CURLY-COATED).

ORIGIN.—The breed is about fifty years old, and probably is a cross of the old English or Irish water-spaniel with setter, collie, or Newfoundland.

USES.—Retrieving wounded game and birds.

* SCALE OF POINTS, ETC.

	Value.		Value.
Skull	10	Feet	5
Nose and jaws	10	Tail	5
Ears and eyes	5	Texture of coat and bareness of face	15
Neck	5	Color	5
Loins and back	10	Symmetry and temperament	10
Quarters and stifles	5		
Shoulders	6	Total	100
Chest	4		
Legs, knees, and hocks	5		

GENERAL APPEARANCE.—A strong, smart dog, moderately low on leg, active, lively, and intelligent.

HEAD.—Long and narrow for length. Ears rather small, set

THE RETRIEVER (BLACK, CURLY-COATED).

low, carried close to head, covered with short curls. Jaws long, strong, free from lippiness. Nose black, with wide-open nostrils. Eyes dark, rather large, showing good temper. Pug eye objectionable.

COAT.— A mass of short, crisp curls from occiput to point of tail; a saddleback or patch of uncurled hair behind shoulders.

COLOR.— Black or liver; a white patch on chest penalizing.

NECK.— Long, graceful, muscular, free from throatiness.

SHOULDERS.— *Very* deep, muscular, obliquely placed; chest not too wide, but deep; body rather short, well ribbed, and muscular.

LEGS AND FEET.— Fore legs straight, bone plenty; not too long, well set under body. Feet round, compact; toes well arched.

LOINS.— Powerful and deep.

TAIL.— Carried pretty straight, and covered with short curls.

WEIGHT.— Dogs, 55 to 68 pounds; bitches, 5 pounds less.

(From *Modern Dogs*.)

THE RETRIEVER (BLACK, FLAT- OR WAVY-COATED).

ORIGIN AND USES same as the black, curly-coated variety.

SCALE OF POINTS, ETC.

	Value.		Value.
Skull	10	Legs, knees, and hocks	10
Nose and jaws	10	Feet	5
Ears and eyes	5	Tail	5
Neck	5	Coat	5
Loins and back	10	Color	5
Quarters and stifles	10	Symmetry and temperament	10
Shoulders	6		
Chest	4	Total	100

HEAD.—Bone at top wide and flat, with furrow down middle; brows not pronounced. Ears small, set low, carried close to head (not hound-like), covered with short hair. Eyes medium size, dark, mild, and intelligent. Nose wide; nostrils open. Jaws strong and long. Teeth level.

THE RETRIEVER (BLACK, FLAT- OR WAVY-COATED).

NECK.—Long enough to allow dog to stoop when trailing; loins and back wide, deep, and strong.

QUARTERS AND STIFLES.—Muscular quarters, with nicely turned stifles.

SHOULDERS AND CHEST.—Shoulders long, sloping; chest deep and broad; ribs well sprung.

LEGS AND FEET.—Legs strong, long, and muscular, clean, and free from lumber; knees broad; hocks well developed and clean. Feet rather large, compact, with well-arched toes; soles thick and strong.

TAIL.—Bushy (not feathery); carried gaily, but not over back.

COAT.—Not so short as the pointer's, close, thick, and straight as possible.

COLOR.—Rich black, free from rustiness and white.

SYMMETRY.—Highly valued, likewise evidence of good temper.

WEIGHT.—Dogs, 50 to 70 pounds; bitches smaller.

LEEDS BARRY.

THE ST. BERNARD (ROUGH-COATED).

ORIGIN.—This is a point of great uncertainty, as the monks of St. Bernard are utterly unable to throw any light on the subject. According to tradition, however, the race sprang from a cross of a bitch of Denmark of the bulldog species, and the mastiff (shepherd-dog) of the Pyrenees. The size comes from the Denmark dog, and the sense of smell from the mastiff. The St. Bernard was first imported into England in 1815.

USES.—An invaluable house-dog, guardian, and companion. Used on the Swiss mountains by the monks to find and succor lost travelers.

* SCALE OF POINTS, ETC.

	Value.		Value.
Head, ears, and eyes	25	Legs and feet	10
Expression and character	15	Coat	10
Neck, shoulders, and chest	10	Color and markings	10
Body	15		
Stern	5	Total	100

THE ST. BERNARD (ROUGH-COATED).

HEAD.—Large, massive, the circumference twice the length; short from stop to tip of nose; full below eye; square muzzle; great depth from eye to lower jaw. Lips deep, not too pendulous. Stop abrupt, well defined, and straight to end of nose. Skull broad, rounded at top, *not* domed; prominent brow. Ears medium size, close to cheek, strong at base, heavily feathered. Eyes rather small, deep set, dark, not too close together; lower eyelid drooping, showing haw. Nose large, black; well-developed nostrils. Teeth level.

EXPRESSION.—Denoting benevolence, dignity, and intelligence.

NECK.—Lengthy, muscular, slightly arched; dewlap developed.

SHOULDERS AND CHEST.—Shoulders broad, sloping; chest wide and deep.

BODY.—Level back, slightly arched over loins; ribs well rounded; loins wide and muscular.

TAIL.—Set on rather high; long, bushy; carried low in repose, slightly above *line* of back when in motion.

LEGS AND FEET.—Fore legs perfectly straight, strong. Hind legs heavy in bone, well bent at hocks; thighs muscular. Feet compact and large; well-arched toes.

SIZE.—Dogs, 30 inches at shoulder; bitches, 27 inches (the taller, the better, if proportioned well). General outline suggests great power and endurance.

COAT.—Dense, flat, rather full around neck; thighs not too heavily feathered.

COLOR AND MARKINGS.—Red, orange, various shades of brindle, or white with patches of above colors. Markings should be: white muzzle and blaze on face, collar around neck; white on chest, fore legs, feet, and end of tail; black shadings on face and ears. If blaze be wide, running through collar, a spot of body-color should be on top of head.

DISQUALIFYING POINTS.

Dudley, liver-colored nose; fawn if whole-colored or with black shadings only; black, black and tan, black and white, black, tan, and white, and all white, though an all white has taken high honors under one of our best judges.

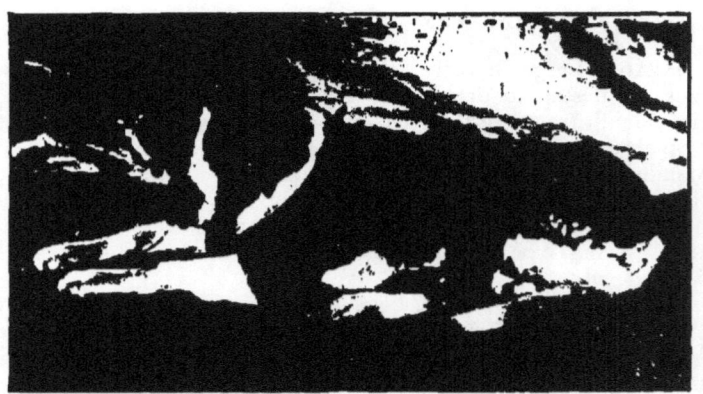

CHAMPION SCOTTISH LEADER.

THE ST. BERNARD (SMOOTH-COATED).

ORIGIN, USES, AND * SCALE OF POINTS are the same as the rough-coated variety, with the exception of the coat, which should be very dense, broken-haired, lying smooth, tough without being rough to the touch, with thighs slightly bushy.

The tail at root is covered with longer and denser hair than on body, the hair gradually growing shorter at the tip; the tail is bushy, but has no feather.

W. J. Comstock's, Providence, R. I.
MIDNIGHT.   DARKNESS.

THE SCHIPPERKE.

ORIGIN.—Wholly Dutch, but how far back it dates is unknown.

USES.—The canal-boatmen in Holland use this "little beggar" as a guard against intruders, as well as to advise the captain of an approaching boat. It will kill rats, swims like a duck, and as a companion is not surpassed.

* SCALE OF POINTS, ETC.

	Value.		Value.
Head, nose, eyes, and teeth	20	Feet	5
Ears	10	Hind quarters	10
Neck, shoulders, and chest	10	Coat and color	20
Back and loins	5	General appearance	10
Fore legs	5		
Hind legs	5	Total	100

GENERAL APPEARANCE.—A small, cobby dog, with sharp expression, lively, always on the alert.

HEAD.—Foxy in type; skull broad, not round; little stop.

Muzzle fine, not weak, well filled out below eyes. Nose black and small. Eyes small, dark brown, not full, more round than oval, bright, and full of expression. Ears moderate length, tapering, carried stiffly erect and at right angles with skull. Teeth strong and level.

NECK.—Short, strong, full, and stiffly arched.

SHOULDERS AND CHEST.—Shoulders muscular, sloping; chest deep and broad.

BACK.—Short, straight, strong; loins powerful and well drawn up.

LEGS AND FEET.—Fore legs perfectly straight, well under body, good bone. Hind legs strong; hocks well let down. Feet small, cat-like; nails black.

HIND QUARTERS.—Fine compared to fore parts, muscular, well developed; rump well rounded; tailless.

COAT.—Black, abundant, dense, harsh; smooth on head, ears, and legs; lying close on back and sides; erect and thick around neck, forming a mane and frill; well feathered on thighs.

WEIGHT.—About 12 pounds.

DEFECTS.

White hairs are objected to.

DISQUALIFYING POINTS.

Drop or semi-erect ears.

J. T. Kent's, 2009 Walnut Street, Philadelphia, Pa.
KENT RODERIGO.

THE SETTER (ENGLISH).

ORIGIN.—Best authorities claim it to be descended from the old Spanish setting-spaniel.

USES.—Hunting all kinds of game-birds.

*SCALE OF POINTS, ETC.

	Value.		Value.
Skull	5	Feet	8
Nose	5	Flag	5
Ears, lips, and eyes	10	Symmetry and quality	10
Neck	5	Coat	5
Shoulders and chest	15	Color	5
Back, quarters, and stifles	15		
Legs, elbows, and hocks	12	Total	100

HEAD.—Considerable prominence of occipital bone, moderately narrow between ears, with decided brow over eyes. Nose long, wide, without fullness under eye; nostrils large and wide apart. Dark specimens should have black nose; for orange and whites, or lemon and whites, a colored nose is desirable. Jaws level, and of equal length. Ears small, shorter than a pointer's, and carried close to cheeks, partly clothed with silky hair; leather thin and soft.

Lips not full nor pendulous. Eyes medium size, animated, best colors being brown.

NECK.—Not throaty; skin rather loose; slightly arched.

SHOULDERS AND CHEST.—Shoulders sloping; elbows well let down; chest deep; ribs well sprung, with great depth of back ribs.

BACK.—Arched over loins, but not wheel-back; stifles well bent, set wide apart.

LEGS, ELBOWS, AND TOES.—Legs straight; arms muscular; knees broad and strong; pasterns short; hind legs muscular, plenty of bone; hocks clean and strong.

FEET.—Either cat- or harefoot; but either must be well clothed with hair and between toes.

FLAG.—Sweeps gently downward; feather plenty, straight and silky.

COAT.—Soft, silky, without curl.

COLOR.—Black and white, ticked with large splashes and more or less marked with black; orange and white, liver and white, ticked as above; black and white, ticked with tan markings; orange or lemon and white; black and white; liver and white.

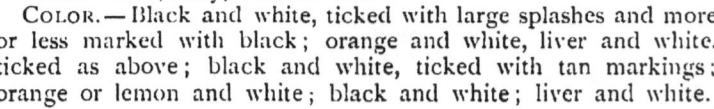

J. R. Oughton's, Dwight, Ill.
HEATHER LAD.

THE SETTER (GORDON).

ORIGIN.—The Duke of Gordon claims to be the originator of this breed (1820), being the outcome of a cross with a breed of setters he then owned, and one of his very keen-nosed collies.

USES.—Hunting all kinds of game-birds.

* SCALE OF POINTS, ETC.

	Value.		Value.
Head and neck	35	Coat and feather	10
Shoulders and chest	12	Tail	5
Loins and quarters	12		
Feet and legs	16	Total	100
Color	10		

HEAD.—Heavier than the English setter's, broad at top between ears; skull slightly rounded; occiput well developed. Nose moderately long and broad across top; nostrils well distended. Some good ones show slight dewlap and haw.

BODY. — Heavier than the English setter's, but may be judged on same lines.

COLOR. — This is of great importance. The colors are black and tan. The black should be jet black (not brown nor rusty); the tan, a rich dark mahogany, grown on inside of thighs, down front of stifles, and on front legs to knees; muzzle also tan; spots over eyes well defined, also those on the points of shoulders.

G. Shippen's, 160 East Thirty-eighth Street, New York.
SHAMROCK O'MORE.

THE SETTER (IRISH).

ORIGIN.—Probably the same as that of the English setter, the color now making it a distinct breed. It was originally red and white.

USES.—Hunting all kinds of game-birds.

* SCALE OF POINTS, ETC.

	Value.		Value.
Head	10	Tail	8
Eyes	5	Coat and feather	8
Ears	5	Color	8
Neck	5	Size, style, and general appear-	
Body	15	ance	14
Shoulders, fore legs, and feet	12		
Hind legs	10	Total	100

HEAD.—Long and lean; skull oval (from ear to ear), with well-defined occipital protuberance; brows raised, showing stop; muzzle moderately deep, fairly square at end; from stop to point of nose should be long; nostrils wide, and jaws of nearly equal length;

flews not pendulous. Color of nose dark mahogany or dark chocolate, that of eyes (which ought not to be too large) rich hazel or brown. Ears of moderate size, fine in texture, set on low, well back, and hanging in a neat fold close to head.

NECK.—Moderately long, very muscular, but not too thick, slightly arched, free from throatiness.

BODY.—Proportionately long; shoulders fine at the points, deep, and sloping well back; chest deep, rather narrow in front; ribs well sprung; loins muscular and slightly arched; hind quarters wide and powerful.

LEGS AND FEET.—Hind legs from hip to hock long and muscular, from hock to heel short and strong; stifles and hock-joints well bent, and not inclined either in or out. Fore legs strong, sinewy, having plenty of bone, with elbows free, well let down, and not inclined either out or in. Feet rather small, very firm; toes strong, close together, and arched.

TAIL.—Moderate length, set on rather low, strong at root, and tapering to a fine point; carried in a slight, simitar-like curve, or straight, nearly level with back.

COAT.—On head, front of legs, and tips of ears short and fine, but on all other parts of body of moderate length, flat, and as free as possible from curl or wave.

FEATHERING.—The feather on upper portion of ears long and silky, on back of fore and hind legs long and fine; a fair amount of hair on belly, forming a nice fringe, which may extend on chest and throat; feet well feathered between toes; tail to have a nice fringe of moderately long hair, decreasing in length as it approaches the point. All feathering as *straight* and flat as possible.

COLOR AND MARKINGS.—Color a rich golden chestnut or mahogany red, with no trace whatever of black; white on chest, throat, or toes, or a small star on forehead, or a narrow streak or blaze on nose or face, *not* to disqualify.

Wilford Kennels, Cohoes, N. Y.
BOXER III.

THE SHEEP-DOG (OLD ENGLISH OR BOBTAIL).

ORIGIN.—It is claimed by the Welsh that this is purely a breed belonging to their own country.

USES.—Same as the rough and smooth varieties of collie.

* SCALE OF POINTS, ETC.

	Value.		Value.
Skull	10	Neck and shoulders	10
Jaw, eyes, and nose	15	Body, loins, and hind quarters	10
Color	10	Coat	10
Teeth and ears	10	Markings	5
Legs (if coated)	10		
Tail (undocked)	10	Total	100

GENERAL APPEARANCE.—Strong, compact, cobby dog, profusely coated all over; moves bear-like.

HEAD.—Skull capacious, rather square; parts over eyes well arched; the whole well covered with hair. Jaw fairly long and square. Stop slightly defined. Eyes in dark blue should be dark brown; in lighter colors they will follow them, and where white predominates a wall eye is typical. Nose black and fairly large. Teeth strong, firm, and even. Ears medium, heavy, and carried close.

NECK AND SHOULDERS.—Neck long, arched, graceful, well coated; shoulders sloping, so that the dog is lower here than at hind quarters.

FORE LEGS.—Straight, plenty of bone, not "leggy," well coated.

FEET.—Round, large, toes arched, pads hard.

TAIL.—All other points being equal, the tailless specimen wins over the one with a tail; the less he has of it, the better.

BODY.—Rather short, very compact; ribs well sprung; brisket deep; loins very stout, arched; hind quarters bulky.

COAT.—Profuse, fairly hard and strong; double-coated, as in the rough collie.

COLOR.—Dark, light, or pigeon blue, and steel gray, generally mixed with white; white collars, legs, chest, and face greatly desired.

HEIGHT.—Twenty inches and upward.

Stonehenge says: "Usually these 'bobs' are strongly made and symmetrical dogs, but without any definite type; they have frequently a tendency to the brindle in color." In awarding prizes, the premier honors seem generally to go to the homeliest specimens.

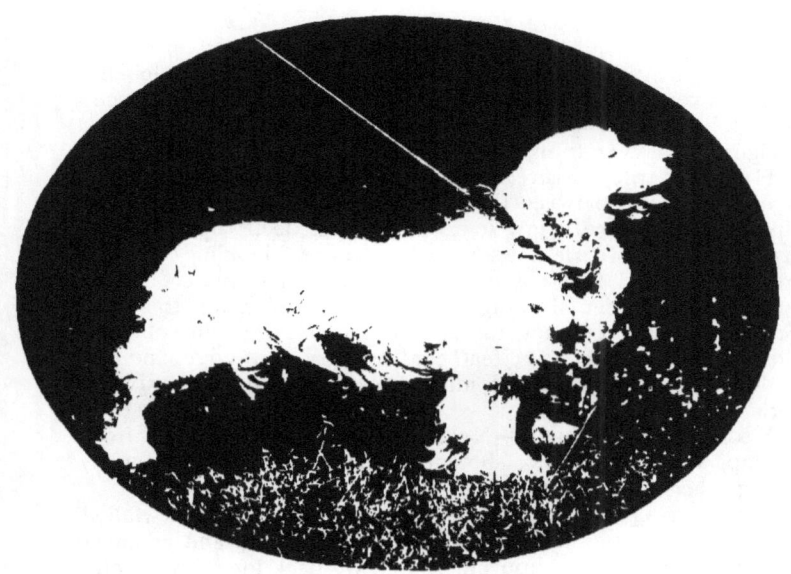

Newcastle Kennels, Brookline, Mass.
FRIAR BOSS.

THE SPANIEL (CLUMBER).

ORIGIN.—It is claimed that this breed originated at Clumber, the seat of the Duke of Newcastle, though records say it was imported by the duke from the kennels of the Duc de Noailles, and possesses a strain of Basset blood. It certainly has some resemblance to that breed of French dogs.

USES.—Hunting game-birds, and generally runs mute.

* SCALE OF POINTS, ETC.

	Value.		Value.
General appearance and size	10	Legs and feet	10
Head	15	Coat and feather	10
Eyes	5	Color and markings	5
Ears	10		
Neck and shoulders	15	Total	100
Body and quarters	20		

GENERAL APPEARANCE AND SIZE.—A long, low, heavy-looking dog, of a very thoughtful expression, betokening great intelligence; should have the appearance of great power, but not clumsiness. Weight of dogs, 55 to 65 pounds; bitches, 35 to 50 pounds.

HEAD.—Large, massive, round above eyes, flat on top, a furrow running up from between the eyes; a marked stop, and large occipital protuberance. Jaw long, broad, and deep; lips of upper jaw overhung. Muzzle not square, but powerful-looking. Nostrils large, open, and flesh-colored, sometimes cherry-colored. Eyes large, soft, deep set, showing haw; hazel in color, not too pale. Ears long, broad at the top, turned over on front edge, vine-shaped, close to head, set on low; feathered only on front edge, and but slightly. Hair short, silky, without slightest approach to wave or curl.

NECK AND SHOULDERS.—Neck long, thick, powerful, free from dewlap, with a large ruff; shoulders immensely strong, muscular, giving a heavy appearance in front.

BODY AND QUARTERS.—Body very long and low, well ribbed up, and long in the coupling; chest of great depth and volume; loins powerful, and not too much arched; back long, broad, and straight, free from droop or bow. Length an important characteristic; the nearer the dog is in length to being two and a half times its height at shoulder, the better. Quarters shapely and very muscular, neither drooping nor stilty.

LEGS AND FEET.—Fore legs short, straight, immensely heavy in bone, well in at elbow. Hind legs heavy in bone, but not as heavy as fore legs; no feather below hocks, but thick hair on back of leg just above foot. Feet large, compact, and plentifully filled with hair between toes.

COAT AND FEATHER.—Coat silky and straight, not too long, extremely dense; feather long and abundant.

COLOR AND MARKINGS.—Color lemon and white, and orange and white; the fewer markings, the better. Perfection is solid lemon or orange ears, evenly marked head, muzzle and leg ticked.

STERN.—Set on level, and carried low.

A. C. Wilmerding's, 165 Broadway, New York.
WATNONG I.

THE SPANIEL (COCKER).

ORIGIN.—Presumably an offshoot of the field-spaniel.
USES.—Hunting, principally woodcock and partridge.

* SCALE OF POINTS, ETC.

	Value.		Value.
General appearance	10	Length	5
Head	15	Legs and feet	15
Eyes	5	Coat	10
Ears	10	Tail	5
Neck and shoulders	10		
Body	15	Total	100

GENERAL APPEARANCE, SYMMETRY, ETC.—A well-built, graceful, and active dog, showing strength without heaviness. Any of the spaniel colors is allowable. (See Field-spaniel.) Weight not over 28 nor less than 18 pounds.

HEAD.—Fair length; muzzle cut off square, tapering gradually from the eye, not snipy; skull rising in a graceful curve from stop, and with same outline at occiput, the curve line being flatter, but still curving at middle of skull. Head should be narrowest at the eyes, and broadest at set-on of ears, and, viewed from the front, outline between ears should be a nearly perfect segment of a circle. Stop is marked, and a groove runs up the skull, gradually becoming less apparent, till lost about half-way to occiput. This prevents the domed King Charles skull, and produces a light, graceful, well-balanced head. Jaws level. Teeth strong, regular. Eyes round and moderately full, corresponding in color with coat. Ears lobular, set on low; leather fine, and not extending beyond nose; well clothed with long, silky hair, which *must* be straight or wavy—no positive curls or ringlets.

NECK AND SHOULDERS.—Neck sufficiently long to allow the nose to reach the ground easily; muscular, and running into well-shaped, sloping shoulders.

BODY.—Ribs well sprung; chest of fair width and depth; body well ribbed back, short in the coupling; flank free from any tucked-up appearance; loins strong; length from tip of nose to root of tail about twice the height at shoulder.

LEGS AND FEET.—Fore legs short, strong in bone and muscle, straight, neither bent in nor out at elbows; pasterns straight, short, and strong; elbows well let down. Hind legs strong; well-bent stifles; hocks straight, and near the ground. Feet of good size, round, turning neither in nor out; toes not too spreading; soles furnished with hard, horny pads, with plenty of hair between the toes.

COAT.—Abundant, soft, and silky, straight or wavy, without curl; chest, legs, and tail well feathered; no topknot nor curly hair on top of head.

TAIL.—Usually docked; carried nearly level with back. At work it is carried lower, with a quick, nervous action which is characteristic of the breed.

Rowland P. Keasbey's, 874 Broadway, New York.
BLACK NIGHT.

THE SPANIEL (FIELD).

ORIGIN.—Probably one of the oldest of the known breeds, coming originally from Spain; in fact, it is claimed as the parent of the setter.

USES.—Hunting game-birds, principally woodcock and partridge.

* SCALE OF POINTS, ETC.

	Value.		Value.
Head	15	Body and quarters	20
Ears	10	Coat and feather	15
Neck	5	Tail	10
Shoulders and arms	10		
Legs and feet	15	Total	100

GENERAL APPEARANCE.—Considerably larger, heavier, stronger in build than the cocker. Conformation should be long and low, more so than the cocker. Colors most preferred are solid black or liver; but liver and white, black and white, black and tan, orange, and orange and white are all legitimate spaniel colors.

HEAD.—Long, and not too wide, carried gracefully; skull

showing clearly cut brows, but without a very pronounced stop; occiput distinct, and rising considerably above set-on of ears. Muzzle long, with well-developed nose, not too thick immediately in front of eye, and maintaining nearly same breadth to the point; sufficient flew to give a certain squareness to muzzle and avoid snipiness. Teeth sound and regular. Eyes intelligent and dark, not showing haw, nor so large as to be prominent or goggle-eyed. Ears long, and hung low on skull, lobe-shaped, and covered with straight or slightly wavy silky feather.

NECK.—Long, graceful, and free from throatiness; not too thick, but strongly set into shoulders and brisket.

SHOULDERS AND ARMS.—Shoulder-blades should lie obliquely, with sufficient looseness of attachment to give freedom to forearms, which should be well let down.

LEGS AND FEET.—Fore legs straight, very strong and short. Hind legs well bent at stifle-joint, with plenty of muscular power. Feet of good size, with thick, well-developed pads; not flat nor spreading.

BODY AND QUARTERS.—Long, with well-sprung ribs; strong, slightly arching loins, well coupled to the quarters, which may droop slightly toward stern.

COAT AND FEATHER.—Coat as straight and flat as possible, silky in texture, of sufficient denseness to afford good protection to the skin in thorny coverts, and moderately long; feather long and ample, straight or very slightly wavy, heavily fringing ears, back of fore legs, between toes, and on back of quarters.

TAIL.—Strong, and not carried higher than level of back.

T. A. Carson's, Kingston, Ontario.
MUSHA.

THE SPANIEL (IRISH WATER).

ORIGIN.—This cannot be traced, yet it is supposed to have a decided cross of the poodle.

USES.—Retrieving wounded game from the water.

* SCALE OF POINTS, ETC.

	Value.		Value.
Head, jaw, eyes, and topknot	20	Feet	5
Ears	5	Stern	10
Neck	5	Coat	15
Body	10	General appearance	10
Fore legs	10		
Hind legs	10	Total	100

GENERAL APPEARANCE.—A strong, somewhat leggy dog.
HEAD.—Skull medium length, rather broad; very little stop

Muzzle long, and broad to end. Eyes dark brown, and very intelligent. Ears long, and covered with curls.

NECK.—Long, slightly arched, and muscular.

BODY.—Fair-sized; barrel well rounded and ribbed up.

NOSE.—Liver-colored, large, and well developed.

SHOULDERS AND CHEST.—Shoulders long and oblique; chest deep, but not very wide.

BACK AND LOINS.—Back strong and flat; loins strong, fair length, and a trifle arched.

HIND QUARTERS.—Long; hocks well let down, and stifles straighter than in other varieties of spaniels.

STERN.—Strong at root, and tapering to a fine point; the hair on it must be quite short, straight, and close-lying.

LEGS AND FEET.—Legs well boned and quite straight, somewhat long. Feet rather large.

COAT.—All over little curls, hard, but not woolly. The topknot of long hair should fall over the eyes in a peak, and legs should have as little feather on them as possible.

COLOR.—A rich, dark liver. White on toes or breast a *defect*, but not a disqualification.

NEGATIVE POINTS.

	Value.
Feather on stern	10
White on chest	5

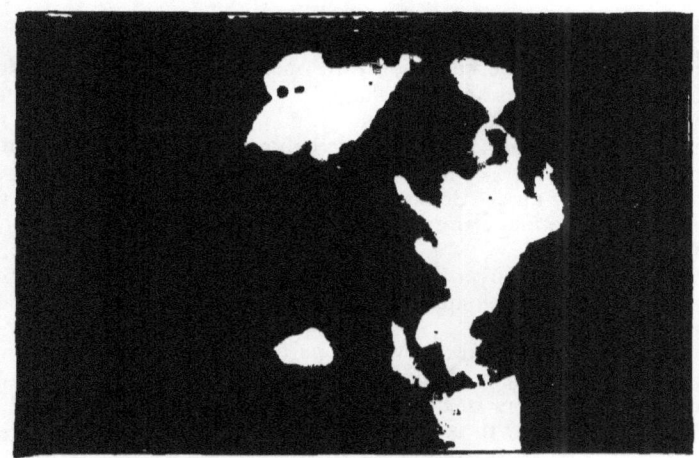

W. J. Burkhardt's, 1301 Broadway, Brooklyn, N. Y.
JINGO.

THE SPANIEL (JAPANESE).

ORIGIN.—A native of Japan, where it is also called the "sleeve-dog," on account of being carried there by the "swells" of that country.

USES.—Simply a pet dog, and extremely intelligent.

SCALE OF POINTS, ETC.

	Value.		Value.
Head—size and shape of skull	10	Size and symmetry	20
Shortness of face and muzzle	10	Legs and feet	10
Width of muzzle	5	Tail	10
Eyes	10		
Ears	10	Total	100
Coat and markings	15		

HEAD AND NECK.—Head large, broad; slightly rounded skull; neck short, and moderately thick. Eyes large, dark, lustrous, rather prominent, wide apart. Muzzle strong, wide, very short from stop to nose; jaws upturned; teeth not to be shown;

nose very short, the end wide with open nostrils, and same color as markings. Ears small, V-shaped; well feathered, set high, and wide apart; carried forward.

BODY.—Compact, squarely built, cobby, the body and legs forming a square.

LEGS AND FEET.—Bones of legs small, slender, well feathered. Feet small, cat-like; the feather increasing the length, *never* the width.

TAIL.—Carried over back in tight curl; profusely feathered.

COAT.—Profuse, long, straight, rather silky, free from wave, not too flat.

COLOR.—Black, red, or white; parti-colors with white ground preferred. Blenheim markings are most showy. In variation of markings the colors *must* remain distinct.

WEIGHT.—Four to nine pounds; the smaller, the better.

Rowland P. Keasbey's, 874 Broadway, New York.
COLESHILL RUFUS.

THE SPANIEL (SUSSEX).

ORIGIN.—It is impossible to trace this origin.
USES.—Hunting pheasants, and sometimes for its fur.

SCALE OF POINTS, ETC.

	Value.		Value.
Head and jaw	15	Feet	5
Eyes	5	Stern	5
Ears	5	Coat and feather	10
Neck	5	General appearance	15
Body	15		
Fore legs	10	Total	100
Hind legs	10		

GENERAL APPEARANCE.—Rather massive and muscular, but with free movements and nice tail action.

HEAD.—Moderately long, massive, with depth in proportion; skull broad, and forehead prominent. Eyes hazel, fairly large, and languishing, not showing haw overmuch. Ears thick, fairly large, lobe-shaped; set moderately low, but relatively not so low as in black or other spaniels; carried close to head, and furnished with wavy hair.

NECK.—Muscular, and slightly arched.

BODY.—Long, with well-sprung ribs; fair depth behind shoulders.

NOSE.—Liver color; muzzle large and square; lips somewhat pendulous; nostrils well developed.

SHOULDERS AND CHEST.—Shoulders oblique; chest deep and wide.

BACK AND LOINS.—Back level and long; loins broad.

HIND QUARTERS.—Strong; thighs muscular, and hocks low down.

STERN.—Docked from 5 to 8 inches; set low; not carried above level of back.

LEGS AND FEET.—Legs short and strong; immense bone, and a slight bend in forearm. Feet large, round, and moderately well feathered, with short hair between toes.

COAT.—Body-coat abundant; flat or slightly waved, with no tendency to curl; moderately well feathered on legs and stern, but clean below hocks.

COLOR.—Dark golden liver; not a light ginger or snuff color, but of a rich bronze tinge, not puce.

WEIGHT.—From 35 to 45 pounds.

(From *Modern Dogs*.)   RUBY SPANIEL.   PRINCE CHARLES SPANIEL.

SPANIELS (TOY)—BLENHEIM, KING CHARLES, PRINCE CHARLES, AND RUBY.

ORIGIN.—Shrouded in mystery. The King Charles spaniel derives its name from the second monarch of that name, and the Blenheim from the family seat of the Duke of Marlborough. The colors were originally black, tan, and white for the first breed, and orange or red and white for the second.

USES.—Essentially pet dogs, though at one time the Blenheim was used for hunting birds.

* SCALE OF POINTS, ETC.

King Charles, Prince Charles, and Ruby.

	Value.		Value.
Symmetry, condition, and size	20	Ears	15
Head	15	Coat and feathering	15
Stop	5	Color	10
Muzzle	10		
Eyes	10	Total	100

Blenheim.

	Value.		Value.
Symmetry, condition, and size	20	Coat and feathering	15
Head	15	Color and markings	15
Stop	5	Spot	5
Muzzle	10		
Eyes	5	Total	100
Ears	10		

HEAD.—Well domed, and in good specimens absolutely semi-globular, sometimes even extending beyond the half-circle, and absolutely projecting over eyes, so as nearly to meet upturned nose.

EYES.—Set wide apart, with eyelids square to line of face, not oblique or fox-like; large, lustrous, very dark in color, so as to be generally considered black; their enormous pupils, which are absolutely of that color, increasing the description.

Mrs. F. Senn's, 278 West Eleventh Street, New York.

STOP.—Well marked as in bulldog, or even more so, some good specimens exhibiting a hollow deep enough to bury a small marble.

NOSE.—Short, well turned up, without any indication of artificial displacement; color of end black, and both deep and wide, with open nostrils.

JAW.—Lower jaw wide, leaving plenty of space for tongue and for attachment of lower lips, which should completely conceal teeth; also turned up or "finished," so as to allow of its meeting end of upper jaw, turned up in a similar way.

EARS.—Long, so as to approach the ground; in an average-sized dog they measure 20 inches from tip to tip, and some reach 22 inches; set low on head; heavily feathered. In this respect the King Charles is expected to exceed the Blenheim, and his ears occasionally extend to 24 inches.

SIZE.—The most desirable size is about 10 pounds.

SHAPE.—In compactness of shape these spaniels almost rival the pug, being decidedly cobby, with strong, stout legs, broad back, and wide chest.

COAT.—Long, silky, soft, and wavy, but not curly. In the Blenheim there should be a profuse mane, extending well down in front of chest. Feather well displayed on ears and feet, where it is so long as to give appearance of their being webbed; also carried well up the backs of the legs. In the King Charles, feather on ears is very long and profuse, exceeding that of Blenheim by an inch or more. The feather on tail (which is about 3½ or 4 inches) should be silky, and from 5 to 6 inches in length, constituting a marked flag of a square shape, and not carried above level of back.

COLOR.—Varies with the breed. The King Charles is a rich,

Mrs. F. Senn's, 278 West Eleventh Street, New York.
KING CHARLES SPANIEL.

glossy black and deep tan, *without white;* tan spots over eyes and on cheeks, and the usual markings on legs, are also required. The Blenheim must on no account be whole-colored, but have a ground of pure, pearly white, with bright, rich chestnut or ruby-red markings evenly distributed in large patches; ears and cheeks red; a blaze of white extending from nose up to forehead, and ending between ears in a crescentic curve; in center of this blaze there should be a clear spot of red, size of a sixpence. The tricolor, or Charles the First spaniel, should have the tan of the King Charles, with markings like Blenheim, in black instead of red, on a pearly white ground; ears and under the tail should also be lined with tan. The tricolor has no spot, that beauty being peculiarly the property of the Blenheim.

The only name by which the tricolor, or black, white, and tan, in future shall be recognized, is Prince Charles.

That in future the all-red toy spaniel be known by name of Ruby spaniel; the color of nose to be black. The points of the Ruby to be same as those of King Charles, differing only in color.

Black-and-tan spaniels with markings of white shall be entered in Prince Charles class, and red spaniels with white markings must go into Blenheim class.

F. H. F. Mercer's, Ottawa, Canada.
WEAVER.

THE TERRIER (AIREDALE).

ORIGIN.—Probably a cross of otter-hound and some of the large breed of terriers. Most numerously found in the valley of the Aire and about Bradford, England.

USES.—A gamy vermin-dog.

* SCALE OF POINTS, ETC.

	Value.		Value.
Head	20	Legs and feet	15
Ears	8	Coat and color	20
Neck, shoulders, and chest	12	Weight	5
Back and loins	15		
Hind quarters and stern	5	Total	100

HEAD.—Skull flat, moderately narrow, tapering slightly to eyes, free from wrinkle. No perceptible stop or indentation between skull and muzzle, except in profile. Jaw long and powerful, free from flews, rather deep, and moderately square at end. Nose black; nostrils large. Mouth level; teeth large and sound. Eyes small, bright, dark in color, with terrier expression. Ears V-shaped, moderate in size and thickness; carried forward as in a fox-terrier; free from long, silky hair.

NECK.—Fair length, gradually widening to shoulders; well carried; free from throatiness.

SHOULDERS AND CHEST.—Shoulders fine, long, and sloping; chest deep, muscular, but neither full nor wide.

BACK AND LOINS.—Back short, straight, and strong; ribs well sprung and rounded; loins broad and powerful, and well ribbed up.

HIND QUARTERS.—Strong, powerful, thick through hams; good muscular second thighs, and stifles fairly bent; no tendency to cow-hocks.

STERN.—Stout and docked; set on rather high, but not raised to a right angle with back.

LEGS AND FEET.—Legs straight and well furnished with bone. Feet round and close, with a good thick sole.

COAT.—Rough or broken; dense and wiry in texture; free from lock or curl.

COLOR.—Dark grizzle back from occiput to end of tail, extending also down sides of body, with dark markings on side of skull; rest of body a good tan, darker on ears than elsewhere.

WEIGHT.—Dogs, 40 to 45 pounds; bitches, 35 to 40 pounds.

DISQUALIFICATIONS.

A Dudley nose; white on throat, face, or feet; white on any other part of body objectionable; a thoroughly bad mouth, i.e., minus a number of teeth, and others cankered; undershot; partial blindness objectionable.

(From *Modern Dogs*.)

THE TERRIER (BEDLINGTON).

ORIGIN.—Supposed both by conformation and color to have sprung from the Dandie Dinmont and otter-hound. The breed is *not* an old one, by any means.

USES.—A gamy vermin-dog.

* No scale of points adopted.

HEAD.—Skull narrow, deep, and rounded, high at occiput; covered with silky tuft or topknot. Jaw long, tapering, sharp, and muscular; little or no stop; lips close-fitting, and no flew. Eyes small and deep set. The blues should have dark eyes; blue and tans, dark, with amber shade; livers, sandies, etc., light brown. Nose small. Blues, and blue and tans, have black noses; livers and sandies, flesh-colored. Teeth level. Ears moderately large, filbert-shaped; carried well forward; flat to cheek; thinly covered, and tipped with fine, silky hair.

LEGS.—Of moderate length, not wide apart, straight, with good-sized, rather long foot.

TAIL.—Thick at root, tapering; slightly feathered; 9 to 11 inches long, and scimitar-shaped.

NECK AND SHOULDERS.—Neck long, deep at base, and rising well from shoulders, which should be flat.

BODY.—Long, flat-ribbed, deep, not wide in chest; slightly arched back, well ribbed; light quarters.

COAT.—Hard, with close bottom, and not lying flat to sides.

COLOR.—Dark blue, blue and tan, liver, liver and tan, sandy, and sandy and tan.

HEIGHT.—Fifteen to sixteen inches.

WEIGHT.—Fifteen to twenty-five pounds.

Rochelle Kennels, New Rochelle, N. Y.
Broomfield Sultan.

THE TERRIER (BLACK-AND-TAN).

ORIGIN.—This breed was until very recently known as the Manchester (England) terrier, and was probably brought into existence by the operatives of that city.

USES.—A gamy vermin-dog, and a nice companion.

* SCALE OF POINTS, ETC.

	Value.		Value.
Head	20	Tail	5
Eyes	10	Color and markings	15
Ears	5	General appearance	
Legs	10	(including terrier quality)	15
Feet	10		
Body	10	Total	100

HEAD.—Long, almost flat, narrow, level, and wedge-shaped, without showing cheek muscles; well filled up under eyes; tapering, tightly lipped jaws; level teeth. Ears, if cropped, must stand perfectly erect; if uncropped, small, thin, and V-shaped, hanging close to head above eyes. Eyes very small, sparkling, and dark, set fairly close together, and oblong in shape. Nose perfectly black.

NECK AND SHOULDERS.—Neck fairly long, tapering from shoulders to head, free from throatiness, slightly arched; shoulders sloping.

CHEST.—Narrow but deep.

BODY.—Moderately short; powerful loins; ribs well sprung; back slightly arched at loins, falling again at joining of tail to same height as the shoulders.

LEGS.—Perfectly straight, set well under body, fair length.

FEET.—More inclined to be cat- than hare-footed; black toe-nails.

TAIL.—Moderately short, thick where it joins body, tapering to a point, not carried higher than the back.

COAT.—Close, smooth, short, and glossy, not soft.

COLOR.—Black and mahogany tan, distributed distinctly over body. On head, tan to the nose; nasal bone jet black; bright spot on each cheek and above each eye. Under jaw and throat are tan; hair inside ear of same color. Fore legs tan to knee, with black lines up each toe and black mark above the foot. Inside hind legs tan, divided with black at hock-joint. Under tail tan, and each side of chest is tanned slightly.

Squantum Kennels, Atlantic, Mass.
HIS NIBS.

THE TERRIER (BOSTON).

ORIGIN.—The parents of this breed were Hooper's Judge (a cross from an English bulldog and an English terrier) and Burnett's Gyp, "a white bitch." The American Kennel Club has now recognized this as a distinct breed. The origin as given dates back to about 1870.

USES.—Purely a toy dog, of very affectionate disposition and equable temper.

* SCALE OF POINTS, ETC.

	Value.		Value.
Skull	12½	Hind legs	4
Ears	5	Feet	2
Eyes	5	Tail	10
Stop	2½	Color	7
Muzzle	12½	Coat	3
Neck	5	General appearance	10
Body	15		
Elbows	2½	Total	100
Fore legs	4		

GENERAL APPEARANCE.—The general appearance is that of a smooth, short-coated, compactly built dog of moderately low stature. The head should indicate a high degree of intelligence and be in proportion to the dog's size; body rather short and well knit; limbs strong and finely turned; no feature being so prominent that the dog appears badly proportioned; all conveying an impression of determination, strength, and activity. Style of a high order, and carriage easy and graceful.

HEAD.—Skull large, broad, and flat, without prominent cheeks, and forehead free from wrinkles. Stop well defined, but indenture not too deep. Eyes wide apart, large and round, neither sunken nor too prominent; color dark and soft. The outside corner should be on a line with cheeks as viewed from the front. Ears small and thin, situated as near corners of skull as possible; rose-ear preferable. Muzzle moderately short, wide, and deep (without wrinkles). Nose black and wide, with a well-defined straight line between nostrils. Jaws broad, square, and even, with short, strong teeth; chops wide and deep, not pendulous, completely covering teeth when mouth is closed.

NECK.—Rather short and thick (without loose skin), and quite well arched.

BODY.—Set moderately low, deep and quite broad at chest, well ribbed up; back quite short, not roached; loins and quarters strong.

ELBOWS.—Set quite low, standing neither in nor out.

FORE LEGS.—Rather wide apart, straight, and well muscled.

HIND LEGS.—Rather straight; quite long from stifle to hock (which should turn neither in nor out); short and straight from hock to pastern. Thighs well muscled. Hocks not too prominent.

FEET.—Small, nearly round, and turned a trifle outward; toes compact and arched.

TAIL.—Moderate in length, set on low, with a moderate downward carriage, fine and tapering, devoid of fringe or coarse hair.

COLOR.—Any color except black, mouse, or liver; brindle and white evenly marked, and whole brindle, are colors most preferred.

COAT.—Fine in texture, short, bright, and not too hard.

WEIGHT.—Light-weight class, 15 to 25 pounds; heavy-weight class, 25 to 35 pounds.

DISQUALIFICATION.

Docked tail.

F. F. Dole's, New Haven, Conn.
GULLY THE GREAT.

THE TERRIER (BULL).

ORIGIN.—This is admittedly a cross between the bulldog and the English terrier.

USES.—Formerly as a fighting dog. Present uses are for vermin, and as a companion it has *no superior*, being kind, gentle, and **exceedingly** honest and loyal.

* THE VARIOUS PARTS OF THE HEAD, BODY, ETC.
SCALE OF POINTS BY RAWDON B. LEE.

	Value.		Value.
Head, including skull, muzzle, lips, jaws, and teeth	25	Back	10
Eyes	10	Legs and feet	15
Ears (badly cropped or otherwise)	5	Coat	10
Neck and shoulders	15	Stern	10
		Total	100

GENERAL APPEARANCE.—The general appearance of the bull-terrier is that of a symmetrical animal, an embodiment of agility, grace, elegance, determination, and good nature.

HEAD. — Long, flat, and wide between ears, tapering to the nose, without cheek muscles; slight indentation down face, without a stop. Jaws long and very powerful; large black nose, and open nostrils. Eyes small and very black. Lips should meet as tightly as possible, without a fold. Teeth regular in shape, *and meet exactly*, any deviation being a great fault. Ears always cropped for the show-bench, and should be done scientifically and according to fashion.

NECK. — Long, slightly arched, nicely set into shoulders, tapering to head, without any loose skin.

BODY. — Shoulders strong, muscular, slanting; chest wide and deep; ribs well rounded.

BACK. — Short, muscular, but not out of proportion.

LEGS. — Fore legs perfectly straight, well-developed muscles; not "out at shoulder," but set on racing lines; very strong at pasterns. Hind legs long, muscular, with good, strong, straight hocks, well let down.

FEET. — Resembling those of the hare.

COLOR. — White.

COAT. — Short, close, stiff to the touch, with fine gloss.

TAIL. — From 10 to 12 inches long, set on very low; thick where it joins the body, tapering to a fine point; carried at an angle of about 45 degrees, without curl, and never over the back.

WEIGHT. — About 30 pounds.

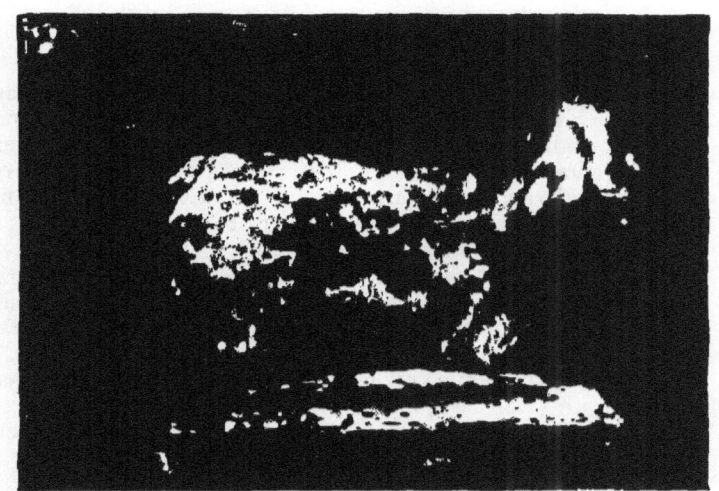

CLYDESDALE LORIS.

THE TERRIER (CLYDESDALE OR PAISLEY).

ORIGIN.—Both are often considered as one breed, and supposed to be of Skye extraction.

USES.—A vermin-dog, but better as a pet.

* SCALE OF POINTS, ETC.

	Value.		Value.
Head	15	Tail	10
Ears	10	Legs and feet	5
Body	15	Style and general appearance	15
Coat	20		
Color	10	Total	100

GENERAL APPEARANCE AND STYLE.—The general appearance is that of a long, low dog with plenty of style, having a rather large head in proportion to its size, and with a coat that looks like silk or spun glass.

HEAD.—Skull slightly domed, very narrow between ears, gradually widening toward eyes, and tapering very slightly to nose; covered with long, silky hair, perfectly straight, without curl or waviness, and extending well beyond nose, plentiful on sides of head, joined by that from the ears, giving head a very large and rather heavy appearance. Muzzle very deep and powerful, tapering very slightly to nose, which should be large and well spread over the muzzle, always black. Jaws strong; teeth perfectly level. Eyes rather wide apart, large, round, moderately full, but not prominent; brown, and expressive of great intelligence.

EARS.—This is a most important point. They should be as small as possible, set on high, carried perfectly erect, covered with long, silky hair, which should hang in a beautiful fringe down side of head, joining that on jaws. (Well-carried, finely fringed ears are one of the greatest points of beauty.)

NECK.— Rather long, very muscular, well set into the shoulders, covered with same class of hair as the body.

BODY.—Very long, deep in chest, well ribbed up; back perfectly level.

COAT.—Very long, perfectly straight, free from curl or waviness; very glossy and silky in texture (not linty), and without any pily under coat.

COLOR.—Dark blue to light fawn, the various shades of blue—dark blue for preference, but without any approach to blackness or sootiness. Color of head, beautiful silvery blue, which gets darker on ears; the back, various shades of dark blue, inclining to silver on lower parts of body and legs. Tail is generally the same shade or a little darker than the back.

TAIL.—Perfectly straight, not too long, carried almost level with back; nicely fringed or feathered.

LEGS AND FEET.—Legs short and straight, well set under body, both legs and feet well covered with silky hair. (In a good specimen the legs are scarcely seen.)

William Wanton Dunnell's.
KELSO COUNT.

THE TERRIER (DANDIE DINMONT).

ORIGIN.—Mentioned in 1800 by Davidson as springing from Tarr, reddish and wire-haired (a bitch), and Pepper (shaggy and light), which shows true terrier blood.

USES.—An essentially vermin-dog, "dead game;" and when a fox, otter, etc., is to be bolted it is unsurpassed. It is a curious fact that when unearthing its game it generally does its fighting on its *back*, tearing and scratching its opponent's throat with tooth and nail.

* SCALE OF POINTS, ETC.

	Value.		Value.
Head	10	Coat	15
Eyes	5	Color	5
Ears	5	Size and weight	10
Neck	5	General appearance	10
Body	20		
Tail	5	Total	100
Legs and feet	10		

HEAD.—Strongly made and large, with muscles well developed; skull broad between ears, growing less toward eyes; forehead well

domed. Head covered with soft, silky hair, not confined to a mere topknot. Cheeks have a gradual taper toward muzzle, which is deep and strong and about 3 inches in length. Muzzle covered with darker hair than topknot, the top part being generally bare for about 1 inch from back of nose, where it is about 1 inch broad. Nose and inside of mouth black or dark-colored. Teeth strong and very large, level in front, the upper ones overlapping the under ones. "Swine mouth" is objectionable, but not so much so as the bulldog mouth. Eyes wide apart, full, large, round, bright, full of determination, set low and prominent, and of a rich, dark hazel. Ears large, pendulous, set well back, wide apart, and low on skull, hanging close to cheek, tapering to a point, the tapering being mostly on the back part. They are covered with soft, straight brown hair (sometimes almost black), with a feather of light hair about 2 inches from tip. The feather does not show, sometimes, till the dog is 2 years old. Leather rather thin. Length of ear 3 to 4 inches.

NECK.—Very muscular and strong, and well set into shoulders.

BODY.—Long, strong, and flexible; ribs well sprung; chest deep: back rather low at shoulder; a slight, gradual droop from loins to root of tail.

TAIL.—Rather short (8 to 10 inches), covered on upper side with wiry hair, darker than on body; a feather of about 2 inches, getting shorter as it nears the tip; simitar-like, not curled nor twisted and when excited carried gaily above the level of the body.

LEGS AND FEET.—Fore legs short, immense muscular development and bones set wide apart; feet well formed, *not* flat. "Bandy legs" objectionable. Hair on fore legs and feet of blue dog should be tan; on a mustard dog a darker shade than on head, which is creamy white. Hind legs are rather longer than front ones, rather wide apart, with feet smaller than front ones, without feather and dew-claws; claws should be dark.

COAT.—Very important. Hair should be 2 inches long, and that from skull to root of tail a mixture of hard and soft hair. The hard hair should be wiry, the coat being pily, that under body being softer and lighter in color than on top.

COLOR.—Pepper or mustard. The pepper ranges from dark blue black to a light silver gray; the mustards from a red brown to pale fawn, the head being creamy white, with legs and feet darker than head. Claws are dark as in other colors. Nearly all Dandies have some white on chest and white claws.

SIZE.—Eight to eleven inches at shoulder. Limit weight, 24 pounds.

LENGTH.—From top of shoulder to root of tail should be twice the dog's height.

August Belmont's.
CHAMPION BLEMTON VICTOR II.

THE TERRIER (FOX, SMOOTH-COATED).

ORIGIN.—Evidently a very judicious cross between a beagle and a bull-terrier.

USES.—Essentially a vermin-dog of the highest order, and capable of worrying a fox when it has taken to earth. It is used by the operatives in some parts of England for coursing rabbits.

* THE VARIOUS PARTS OF THE HEAD, BODY, ETC.
SCALE OF POINTS BY RAWDON B. LEE.

	Value.		Value.
Head, jaws, and ears	20	Legs and feet	15
Neck	5	Coat	10
Shoulders and chest	10	Size, symmetry, and character	20
Back and loins	10		
Stern and hind quarters	10	Total	100

HEAD.—Skull flat, moderately narrow, gradually decreasing in width to eyes. Not much stop, but there should be more dip

in profile between forehead and top jaw than in the greyhound. Cheeks must *not* be full. Ears V-shaped, small, of moderate thickness, drooping forward close to cheek, not hanging by side of head. Jaws strong and muscular, of fair punishing strength. There should not be much falling away below eyes. This part of head should be moderately chiseled out, but not like a wedge. Nose tapering and black. Eyes dark, small, rather deep set, full of fire and intelligence; nearly circular in shape. Teeth nearly level.

NECK.—Clean, muscular, without throatiness, of fair length, and gradually widening to shoulders.

SHOULDERS AND CHEST.—Shoulders long and sloping, well laid back, clearly cut at withers; chest deep and not broad.

BACK.—Short, straight, and strong, with no appearance of slackness.

LOINS.—Powerful and very slightly arched. Fore ribs moderately arched; back ribs deep. The dog should be well ribbed up.

HIND QUARTERS.—Strong, muscular, quite free from droop or crouch; thighs long and powerful; hocks near the ground.

STERN.—Set on rather high, carried gaily, but *not* over back or curled; of good strength, anything approaching a "pipe-stopper" tail being especially objectionable.

LEGS.—Straight, showing little or no appearance of ankle in front; strong in bone, short and straight in pastern. Both fore and hind legs carried straight forward in traveling; stifles not turning outward; elbows perpendicular to the body.

FEET.—Round, compact, not large; soles hard and tough; toes moderately arched, and turned neither in nor out.

COAT.—Smooth, flat, hard, dense, and abundant. Belly and under side of thighs should not be bare.

COLOR.—White should predominate; brindle, red, or liver markings are *objectionable*.

SYMMETRY, SIZE, AND CHARACTER.—The dog must present a generally gay, lively, and active appearance. Bone and strength in a small compass, but this does not mean that a fox-terrier should be cloggy or in any way coarse. Speed and endurance must be looked to as well as power, and the symmetry of the foxhound taken as a model. The terrier must on no account be leggy, nor must it be too short in leg. It should stand like a cleverly made hunter, covering a lot of ground, yet with a short back.

WEIGHT is not a certain criterion of a terrier's fitness for its work; general shape, size, and contour are the main points; it should not scale over 20 pounds in show condition.

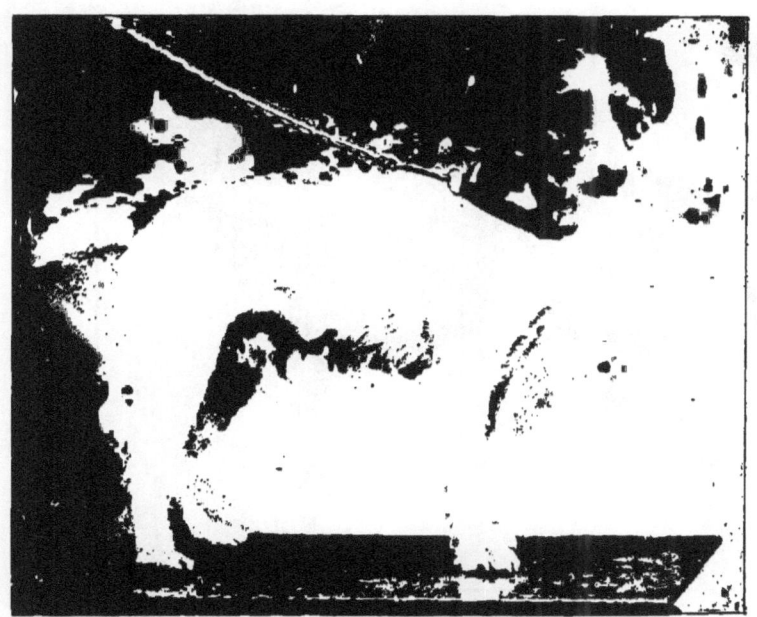

G. M. Carnochan's, 46 Exchange Place, New York.
THORNFIELD KNOCKOUT.

THE TERRIER (FOX, WIRE-HAIRED).

With the exception of the coat, which should be broken, the origin, uses, and scale of points of this breed are identical with the smooth-coated variety.

The harder and more wiry the texture of the coat is, the better. The dog should not look nor feel woolly, and there should be no silky hair. The coat should not be too long, but it should show a marked difference from the smooth species.

W. J. Comstock's, Providence, R.
DUNMURRY.

THE TERRIER (IRISH).

ORIGIN.—Mr. George R. Krehl, editor of the London (England) "Stockkeeper" and English vice-president of the Irish Terrier Club, says this is a true and distinct breed, indigenous to Ireland, and that no man can trace its origin, which is lost in antiquity.

USES.—Rabbiting, and as a vermin-dog.

* SCALE OF POINTS, ETC.

	Value.		Value.
Head, jaws, teeth, and eyes	15	Hind quarters and stern	10
Ears	5	Coat	15
Legs and feet	10	Color	10
Neck	5	Size and symmetry	10
Shoulders and chest	10		
Back and loins	10	Total	100

Negative Points.

White nails, toes, and feet	10	Coat shaggy or curly	10
Much white on chest	10	Uneven in color	5
Ears cropped	5		
Mouth undershot	10	Total	50

HEAD.—Long; skull flat, rather narrow between ears, free from wrinkle; stop hardly visible. Jaws strong, muscular, but not too full in cheek, and of good punishing length. There should be a slight falling away below the eye, so as not to have a greyhound appearance. Hair on face same description as on body: short (about ¼ inch long), almost smooth and straight; a slight beard is permissible, and that is characteristic. Teeth strong and level. Lips not so tight as a bull-terrier's, but well fitting. Nose black. Eyes dark hazel, small, not prominent, full of life, fire, and intelligence. Ears, when uncut, small and V-shaped, of moderate thickness, set well up, dropping forward close to cheek, free from fringe, and hair thereon shorter and generally darker in color than the body.

NECK.—Fair length, gradually widening toward shoulders, free from throatiness, with a slight sort of frill at each side of neck, running nearly to corner of ear, which is characteristic.

SHOULDERS AND CHEST.—Shoulders *must* be fine, long, sloping; chest deep, muscular, but neither full nor wide.

BACK AND LOINS.—Body moderately long; back strong, straight, with no appearance of slackness; loins broad, powerful, slightly arched; ribs fairly sprung, rather deep than round.

HIND QUARTERS.—Well under the dog, strong, muscular; thighs powerful; hocks near the ground; stifles not much bent.

STERN.—Generally docked, free from fringe or feather; set on pretty high; carried gaily, but not over back, nor curled.

FEET AND LEGS.—Feet strong, tolerably round, moderately small; toes arched, neither turned out nor in; black toe-nails. Legs moderately long, well set on, perfectly straight, plenty of bone and muscle; pasterns short and straight; fore and hind legs moving straight forward when traveling; stifles not turned outward; legs free of feather, and covered with hair as on head.

COAT.—Hard, wiry, not soft nor silky, not so long as to hide outlines of body; straight, flat, no shagginess, no lock nor curl.

COLOR.—"Whole-colored," the most preferable being bright red, wheaten, yellow, and gray; *brindle disqualifying*. White sometimes appears on chest and feet; more objectionable on the latter.

SYMMETRY.—The dog must present an active, lively, lithe, and wiry appearance; lots of substance, free of clumsiness, and framed on the "lines of speed."

TEMPERAMENT.—The Irish terrier, as a breed, is remarkably good-tempered, notably so with mankind, it being admitted, however, that it is perhaps a little too ready to resent interference on part of other dogs, hence called "daredevils."

WEIGHT.—Sixteen to twenty-four pounds.

DISQUALIFICATIONS.

Nose cherry or red; brindle color.

Mrs. J. P. Wade's, Corona, L. I.
FLOSSIE.

THE TERRIER (MALTESE).

ORIGIN.—Indigenous to the island of Malta, and spoken of by Aristotle, B.C. 370, as the lap-dog of the fashionable Greeks and Romans.

USES.—A pet dog essentially.

SCALE OF POINTS, ETC.

	Value.		Value.
Size	15	Ears	5
Coat	15	Legs and body	10
Color	15	Symmetry	10
Color of eyes	10		
Color of nose	10	Total	100
Tail	10		

As no standard is adopted, the following is the description of the dog.

WEIGHT.—Five pounds; limit, seven pounds.

COLOR.—All white, with long, silky hair, looking like spun glass, straight, *not* curly, length *not* less than 7 inches.

HEAD AND BODY.—Nose and eyes black. Tail turned or doubled into coat on back. Ears small, drooping, well clad with hair. Mouth level; teeth white. Black-coated specimens are *very* rare and desirable.

DEFECT.

Ears with fawn markings.

Newcastle Kennels, Brookline, Mass.
BELLINGHAM BAILIFF.   BONNY C.

THE TERRIER (SCOTTISH).

ORIGIN.—Nothing definite of this breed can be traced, though it was for years known in Scotland as the Skye terrier.

USES.—Unearthing vermin, badgers, foxes, etc.

* SCALE OF POINTS, ETC.

	Value.		Value.
Skull	7½	Tail	2½
Muzzle	7½	Coat	15
Eyes	5	Size	10
Ears	5	Color	2½
Neck	5	General appearance	10
Chest	5		
Body	15	Total	100
Legs and feet	10		

GENERAL APPEARANCE.—The face should bear a very sharp, bright, and active expression, and head carried up. The dog should look compact and be possessed of great muscle in his hind quarters. A Scottish terrier *cannot be too powerfully* put together.

HEAD.—Skull long, slightly domed, covered with short, hard hair about ¾ inch long or less; skull not quite flat. Muzzle very powerful, tapering toward nose, which should be black and of good size; jaws level; teeth square, though the nose projects somewhat over the mouth. Eyes wide apart, dark brown or hazel, small and piercing. Ears very small, prick or half prick, sharp-pointed, the hair not long, and free from any fringe on top.

NECK.—Short, thick, muscular; strongly set on sloping shoulders.

CHEST.—Broad and proportionately deep.

BODY.—Moderate length, rather flat-sided, well ribbed up, and exceedingly strong in hind quarters.

LEGS AND FEET.—Legs short, and very heavy in bone, the front ones being straight or slightly bent, and well set on under body; hocks bent; thighs very muscular; feet strong, small, and thickly covered with short hair.

TAIL.—About 7 inches long, carried with a slight bend, and *never* cut.

COAT.—Rather short (about 2 inches), intensely hard, wiry, and very dense.

SIZE.—About 16 pounds for a dog; 14 pounds for a bitch.

COLORS.—Steel or iron gray, brindle, black, red, wheaten, yellow, or mustard color. *White markings are most objectionable.*

HEIGHT.—Nine to twelve inches.

FAULTS.

Large or light eyes; silky or curly coat.

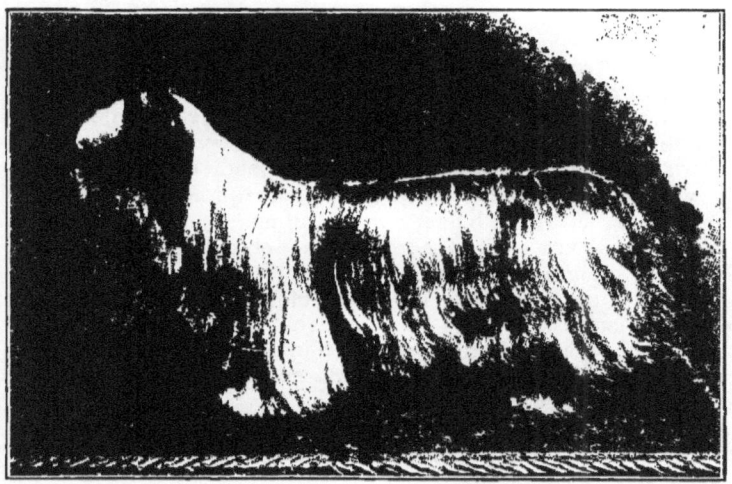

(From *Ladies' Kennel Journal*.)
LAIRD DUNCAN.

THE TERRIER (SKYE).

ORIGIN.—Entirely lost. Indigenous, no doubt, to Scotland.
USES.—A good, gamy vermin-dog, hardy and tough.

* SCALE OF POINTS, ETC.

	Value.		Value.
Size	15	Legs	10
Head	15	Coat	20
Ears	10	Color	5
Body	15		
Tail	10	Total	100

HEAD.—Long; powerful jaws, incisors closing level, or upper jaws just fitting under. Skull wide at front of brow, narrowing between ears, tapering to muzzle, with little falling in between or behind eyes. Eyes hazel, medium size, close set. Muzzle black. Ears, when pricked, not large; erect at outer edges, slanting toward each other inward. When pendent, larger, hanging straight, and flat and close at front.

BODY.—Preëminently long and low; shoulders broad; chest deep; ribs well sprung, oval-shaped, giving flat appearance to sides. Hind quarters full and well developed. Back level, and declining from top of hip to shoulders. Neck long and well crested.

TAIL.—When hanging, upper half perpendicular, under half thrown backward in a curve. When raised, a prolongation of outline of back, not rising higher nor curling up.

LEGS AND FEET.—Legs short, straight, muscular, no dew-claws. Feet large, pointing forward.

COAT (DOUBLE).—Under coat short, close, soft, and woolly; and over coat long (5½ inches), hard, straight, flat, free from crisp or curl. Hair on head shorter, softer, veiling forehead and eyes; on ears, overhanging inside, falling down, not heavily, but surrounding ear like fringe; tail also feathered.

COLOR.—Dark or light blue, or gray or fawn with black points.

HEIGHT AND LENGTH.—Height at shoulder 9 inches; length, occiput to root of tail, 22½ inches.

WEIGHT.—Dogs, 18 pounds; bitches, 16 pounds.

DISQUALIFICATIONS.

Doctored ears or tail; weight over 20 pounds; over- or undershot jaws.

TERRIERS (TOY).

Toy terriers are judged by the same points as the large specimens of the same breed.

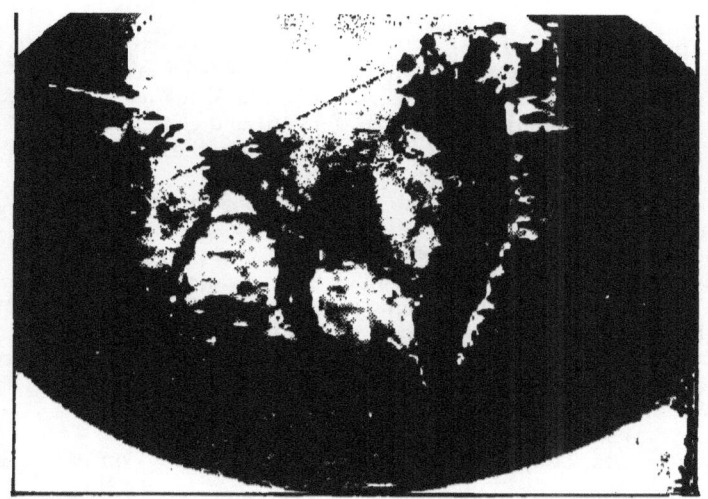

John Brett's, Closter, N. J.
TORY II.

THE TERRIER (WELSH).

ORIGIN.—Claimed by some to be of Welsh origin, by others of English origin. However that may be, the breed was only recognized by the English Kennel Club in 1886, and catalogued under title of "Welsh or English wire-haired black-and-tan terriers."

USES.—Essentially a vermin-dog, "dead game."

* SCALE OF POINTS, ETC.

	Value.		Value.
Head	20	Coat	15
Neck and shoulders	10	Color	10
Body	10	Symmetry	10
Loins and hind quarters	10		
Legs and feet	15	Total	100

HEAD.—Skull flat, rather wider between ears than the wire-haired fox-terrier. Jaws powerful, clean cut, rather deeper and more punishing—giving head a more masculine appearance than that usually seen on a fox-terrier. Stop not too defined; fair length from stop to end of nose. Nose black. Ears V-shaped, small, not too thin, set on fairly high, carried forward and close to cheek. Eyes small, not too deeply set in nor protruding, dark hazel, expressive, and indicating abundant pluck.

NECK.—Moderate length and thickness, slightly arched and sloping.

BODY.—Back short, well ribbed up; loins strong; good depth and moderate width of chest; shoulders long, sloping, well set back; hind quarters strong; thighs muscular; hocks moderately straight, and well let down. Stern set on moderately high, and not too gaily carried.

LEGS AND FEET.—Legs straight, muscular, good bone, strong pasterns. Feet cat-like.

COAT.—Wiry, hard, very close, and abundant.

COLOR.—Black or grizzle and tan, free from pencilings on toes.

SIZE AND WEIGHT.—Fifteen inches in dogs; average weight, 20 pounds.

L. A. Van Zandt's, New City, N. Y.
TOMMY ATKINS II.

THE TERRIER (WHITE ENGLISH).

ORIGIN.—Wholly unknown, but the greatest number come from Manchester (England).

USES.—A very companionable gamy dog.

* SCALE OF POINTS, ETC.

	Value.			Value.
Head	20	Stern		10
Eyes and expression	15	Symmetry		10
Neck and shoulders	10	Size		10
Legs, feet, and chest	15			
Coat	10	Total		100

HEAD.—Narrow, long, level, almost flat; skull wedge-shaped, well filled below eyes, not lippy. Eyes small, black, oblong, and set fairly close. Nose black. Ears cropped and standing perfectly erect.

NECK AND SHOULDERS.—Neck fairly long, tapering; shoulders sloping, no throatiness, slightly arched at occiput.

BODY.—Chest narrow, deep; body short, curving upward at loins; ribs well sprung.

LEGS AND FEET.—Legs perfectly straight, well under body, moderate bone; feet cat-like.

TAIL.—Moderate length, and set on where arch of back ends; thick where it joins body, tapering, and *not* carried higher than the back.

COAT.—Close, hard, short, glossy.

COLOR.—Pure white; colored markings disqualify.

WEIGHT.—Limit, 20 pounds; 14 pounds preferable.

Mrs. F. Senn's, 278 West Eleventh Street, New York.
DUKE OF GAINSBORO.

THE TERRIER (YORKSHIRE).

ORIGIN.—This dog's home is Manchester (England), where it is said to have been originated, the black-and-tan, Skye, and Maltese terriers all being credited with its paternity. Except in color, it resembles greatest the latter dog.

USES.—Essentially a toy dog, beautiful and aristocratic.

* SCALE OF POINTS, ETC.

	Value.		Value.
Quantity and color of hair on body	25	Ears	5
		Legs and feet	5
Quality of coat	15	General appearance	10
Tan	15	Tail	5
Head	10		
Eyes	5	Total	100
Mouth	5		

GENERAL APPEARANCE.—A long-coated, well-proportioned pet dog; coat straight and hanging evenly down each side, parted from nose to end of tail; very compact in form, neat, sprightly, and bearing an important air.

HEAD.—Rather small, flat, not too round in skull, broad at muzzle; black nose. Hair on muzzle very long, of bright golden tan, unmixed with dark or sooty hair. Hair on sides of head very long, and of deeper tan than on center of head. Eyes medium in size, not prominent, dark, with intelligent expression; edges of eyelids dark. Ears cut or uncut, quite erect; if not cut, V-shaped, small, and erect, covered with short hair; color deep tan. Mouth *even;* teeth sound; a loose tooth or two not objectionable.

BODY.—Very compact, good loins, and level on top of back.

COAT.—Hair as long and straight as possible, *not* wavy; glossy, like silk, *not* woolly; extending from back of head to root of tail. Color bright steel blue, not intermingled with fawn, light or dark hairs.

LEGS AND FEET.—Legs quite straight; hair on same a bright golden tan, a shade lighter at ends than at roots. Feet round as possible; toe-nails black.

WEIGHT.—Divided, viz., under 5 pounds, over 5 pounds; limit, 12 pounds.

W. J. Comstock's, Providence, R. I.
MARY.

THE WHIPPET.

ORIGIN.—On account of it being little else than a small English greyhound, its origin is traced to that breed, by which standard it is judged.

USES.—Occasionally for coursing rabbits, but chiefly for trials of speed of about 200 yards. The dogs are run in couples, the waving of a handkerchief or other cloth being the incentive to run.

HEIGHT.—At shoulders about 18 inches.

TREATMENT OF THE DOG IN HEALTH.

FIRST PRINCIPLES.

TEACH your dog to obey you through kindness if possible, *but teach it.* Remember always that it has as much feeling as the average human being, and wonders can be worked through kindness. Rather than strike it with a whip, strike *at* it, the swish of the whip generally having about as much effect as a well-delivered "strike."

The next duty is to teach the dog to be clean about the house. Should it forget itself, make its nose well acquainted with the "offense," rubbing it as hard as you please, "warm its jacket" well, and then turn it out of doors with a well-delivered slap on the body. A repetition of the "moral suasion" act is rarely necessary. In the morning let it out of the house into the yard the first thing you do, and repeat it the last thing before retiring; it will soon learn to understand the meaning of all this and cease to cause trouble. Patience—and sometimes a great deal of it, too—is required to make the dog "well mannered," but perseverance will achieve the desired result. NEVER strike a dog on the head; the body presents sufficient surface.

BREAKING TO CHAIN.

Some dogs take kindly to instruction in this regard, others revel against it. Put a collar on the dog several days before you intend breaking it to chain. Try conscientiously the coaxing process *first;* if it fails, then nothing remains but to drag the dog along till from fear of choking it is forced to follow. Once having undertaken it, *don't stop till you have accomplished your object.* This treatment should not in stubborn cases last over half an hour, though sometimes heavy and headstrong dogs may require two hours. In the majority of cases after half an hour's teaching the dog will lead "steady by jerks," and in a couple of days will become used to the chain. If, however, after a week's experience it tugs and pulls on the lead, use a slip-noose collar, which tightens as the strain grows greater. Choking off its wind when it pulls hard, it will soon grow weary and act rationally. Should this treatment still prove inefficient, some people resort to the spike collar, which, however, should be used only *with the greatest judgment*. No one ever treated his dogs more kindly than I, yet, though I never had a dog upon which it became necessary to use a spike collar, still, perhaps I *would* have used one rather than have my shoulder pulled out of its socket by a dog which I took out for companionship. I would use it only as a *last resort*, and then with the utmost caution.

Feeding.

The dog in its wild state is nearly, if not wholly, carnivorous, but when domesticated becomes omnivorous and therefore thrives best on a mixed diet of bread, meat, and vegetables. Excepting when training or hunting your dogs, a purely meat diet is not desirable any more than it would be for a human being. While its stomach has the power to digest bones, gristle, etc., through the excessive secretions of gastric juices, still it is very easily deranged, and when so affected it may take days for it to resume its normal state; hence expel the thought that any kind of food is "good enough for a dog."

Avoid giving very much corn-meal, as it is too heating and is not possessed of much strength-giving qualities. Let the diet, whether it is for a St. Bernard or a fox-terrier, be a mixture of meat (boiled tripe and mutton are excellent) cooked till it is in shreds, oatmeal, barley, rice, carrots, bread, potatoes, cabbage, or any other vegetable added so as to make the whole thick, and rendered palatable by a goodly supply of salt. Avoid giving chop, steak, or fowl bones, as they are apt to splinter, and, lodging in the intestines, very frequently cause death. Give plentifully of large, soft bones (such as knuckles), which are easily chewed, as they act as a sort of tooth-brush, and aid digestion greatly. Scraps of all sorts from the table tend *best* to preserve the dog's health.

For toy dogs well-cooked rice, finely chopped boiled tripe, *warm* milk, and *lean* meat scraps from the table, mixed with vegetables, should form the common diet. As these dogs are very light eaters, they may be fed three times a day, care being exercised that they do not overload their stomachs at any time.

Sweets of all kinds are objectionable. Unlike the human stomach, the dog's needs much rest; so in the morning feed "just a crumb" and at night let it eat all it desires. A little flour of sulphur or powdered magnesia (a quarter-teaspoonful) now and again will do no harm. Constant and free access to *fresh, clean* water *must* not be neglected. As soon as the dog has eaten all it desires, take the uneaten food away, and do not let it remain to be nibbled at during the day or night.

Boiled liver is an admirable alterative, and one good meal of it should be fed *at least once a week*. If you find your dog has no appetite, don't try to coax or force it, but cease to offer it any food whatever for at least twenty-four hours. A fast of forty-eight hours *will do it no harm* in such cases, and total abstinence often wards off sickness. Should it be disposed to eat grass or horse-droppings, don't try to prevent it, as both are nature's mild remedy for a disordered stomach. In short, feed your dog as you would a human being, and the result will be satisfactory. The feeding of meat does not in any way affect the scenting powers of a dog, nor does it produce worms, distemper, or kindred diseases, as so often stated. Having used the foregoing diet both at home, with my favorite dog, and at my kennels, where I have had as many as ninety at one time, my experience with it for twenty years convinces me that it cannot be improved upon, whether used for a single dog or an entire pack.

Puppies from time of weaning up to six months of age should be fed *four* times daily, from six to nine months three times, and after that age feed same as grown dogs; they too thrive best on diet as already described. Fresh raw minced meat is good, especially for puppies; it strengthens them and tones the stomach. Give freely of fresh milk and buttermilk, especially the latter, as it keeps the stomach sweet.

When puppies are about three weeks old they should be taught to lap scalded milk (sweetened a little) by gently putting their noses into it. They will instinctively lick it off, and after a few lessons will soon lap eagerly. This is always a great relief to a nursing mother, especially where the pups are vigorous or the litter large. A little bread or rice added when they are about four weeks old will do them a vast deal of good. Remember always, if you want strong, healthy dogs, that as puppies they should be fed nutritious food.

Bitches in whelp and while nursing pups should be fed on a soft or mushy diet, such as soups, porridge, etc., as it produces more and better milk, and often prevents fevers.

If you accompany your dogs to a show, and they are not accustomed to the usual food given there, it is always best to give them scraps from a neighboring restaurant, as some dog-biscuits cause excessive purging. There, too, they frequently become very nervous, lose their appetites, and often take cold, resulting in fevers; so it is not a bad scheme during a show to give your setters, for instance, one grain powdered quinine twice a day (smaller or larger dogs in proportion) during the entire show and for some days after it is over. It has been tried with most beneficial results.

VALUE OF EXERCISE.

All dogs, whether large or small, should have exercise, and plenty of it, in order to aid digestion, keep the heart and lungs in good action, and thereby insure a good appetite. Puppies, as is natural to them, take plenty of exercise; but it is when they are grown up that care should be taken that they do not become sluggish and so pave the way to obesity, which tends to affect the coat, digestion, and general appearance. The small varieties will generally of themselves keep "on the go," but mastiffs, setters, and such other large dogs are not always disposed to move about much of their own free will; hence make them the companions of your walks. It is twofold in its good results: it makes you understand each other better, and does the dog no end of good. Bitches in whelp should have plenty of gentle exercise.

WASHING AND GROOMING.

Do not wash your dogs too often, as it removes the natural oil and consequently the gloss, which is so much desired. Careful and *daily* brushing with a dandy-brush, followed by a rubbing down with mittens made of chamois leather, will keep a dog's coat in wonderfully fine condition and *for a long while*. The hound gloves are found to be of great value with smooth-coated dogs, such as Great Danes, pointers, bull-terriers, etc. In the long-haired classes use a brush with one-and-a-half-inch bristles, and a comb with teeth very short and wide apart, not unlike a barber's comb. When washing, best results are attained with *pure* Castile soap, and after rinsing off the dog then using the *imported* German green soft soap. The latter seems to restore the gloss, is better than using eggs, and does not leave the hair so dry. *Don't* wash your dog within two hours after feeding, and when you do it, *do it as quickly as possible*, using *lukewarm* water. Exercise the dog freely *after* it has been well dried. Towels made of salt-sacks are the best for drying purposes.

Great care should be taken in washing Yorkshires and toy spaniels, as, their coats being soft, they hold the dampness even after they appear to be thoroughly dry. The best and safest mode is as follows: Place the dog in a little foot-tub of lukewarm water deep enough to reach to its elbows, and cover the body with soap-suds, *never* putting the soap on the coat. With a soft hair-brush of long bristles brush the hair with the suds, always brushing from the center *downward*, thus reaching all parts of the body, *including the head*. When the dog is cleaned gently force all the suds and water out by smoothing the hair as instructed in brushing, then lift it into another tub of clean lukewarm water and with a soft sponge rinse well. Stand the dog on a table, envelop the body in a soft towel or cloth, and gently press the hands over it until the water and moisture are all absorbed by the cloth. *Never* ruffle or rub the hair; simply smooth it.

Now with a comb of short and widely separated teeth comb out the hair, and with about three brushes, always kept dry by being laid before the fire, brush the hair till it is perfectly dry. Then lay the dog before the fire, where it will be *very* warm, thus insuring it from catching cold. Such prominent breeders as Senn, Burkhardt, *et al.*, dry their dogs in an oven made especially for the purpose.

After the dog is thoroughly dried, brush it, let it run about the house for an hour or so, and then let it rest on a *linen*-covered cushion, which is far better than velvet or plush, as the coat does not adhere to it. A very little fine oil in the palm of the hand rubbed over the coat will generally restore the gloss after washing.

FLEAS.

The bane of a dog's existence is fleas. They are especially troublesome to puppies, worrying them till they become fretful, causing them to irritate the skin and tear their coats through scratching, seeking relief from itching. In addition, where fleas are particularly numerous on a dog they will often so affect it that its appetite is impaired and its digestive organs affected by worriment.

Carbolic soaps will kill these pests, also destroy the hair if constantly used; therefore the greatest permanent relief is found in using a powder. The best results can be attained by taking the dog into the yard or street, dusting it thoroughly with P. D. Q. Compound Powder, rubbing it well into the skin, when both fleas and nits will cease to exist. It is not injurious either to the dog or its hair, and if used on furniture or carpets will prove equally efficacious.

KENNELING.

If you desire to kennel your dog out of doors, *remember always* that it can stand almost any amount of cold, *provided* its kennel is *clean* and *dry* and elevated about six inches above the ground. The elevation allows a free circulation of air and prevents the bottom of the kennel from getting damp and remaining so. The boards should be tongued and grooved so as to shut out all drafts. Provided always with clean, dry straw, the dog will thrive. Foul and damp bedding produces mange, rickets, distemper, rheumatism, etc. If possible avoid keeping the dog on chain, as it frets and irritates it and is very apt to sour its disposition.

Preparing a Dog for Exhibition.

To show a dog "for all there is in him," its coat should be in perfect condition, free from all dead hair, and in the form as called for in the standard pertaining to its special breed. The body should be round, the ribs well covered; and in sporting and large specimens the muscles should be well developed and hard. Where two exhibits about equal in points of conformation come together in the judging ring, the one shown in the best "condition" will receive the blue ribbon. Grooming in the smaller breeds is generally "nine points" toward conditioning.

TREATMENT OF THE DOG IN SICKNESS.

In sickness the patient should *always* receive the very kindest treatment and be spoken to very gently. Rough or harsh handling is peculiarly hurtful where affections are of a nervous character.

When exhaustion is very great, and the patient absolutely refuses to eat, soft, nutritious food should be forced down the throat by first placing it in the mouth, then closing the jaws gently yet firmly, and softly rubbing the windpipe with the hand, thus causing the patient to swallow. Strange to relate, almost any sick dog will eagerly eat meat which has been masticated by its attendant. Warmth and perfect quiet are great factors of a complete and early recovery.

When convalescent the patient should have soft, nourishing food (beef-tea and rice, etc.), and whenever meat is given it should be hashed or cut as fine as possible.

A little port-wine can *always* be given in this description of food with beneficial results. Food should be administered in small quantities and at short intervals.

Bruises, Sprains, Etc.

Spirits of turpentine
" hartshorn
Laudanum
Rape-oil

Mix equal parts of above, forming a liniment, and anoint parts affected. Where an abrasion exists, touch it with friars' balsam, and rub liniment *around* the broken skin, *not on* it.

Burns.

Use equal parts of linseed-oil and lime-water, applying it freely and as soon after the accident as possible.

Canker of the Ear.

Internal canker is an inflammation of the lining membrane of the passage to the ear, accompanied sometimes with suppuration, and when of long standing has a most offensive-smelling discharge. A mangy affection of the ear is often confounded with, or supposed to be, an external canker.

Symptoms.—The ear is very red, inflamed, and heated. The dog continually scratches it, shaking the head as if to remove something from it. After syringing the ear well with warm water and Castile soap, use the following remedy twice daily, holding the dog's head sidewise on the lap and gently pouring a little into the ear.

Goulard's extract of lead	$\frac{1}{2}$ oz.
Glycerin and carbolic acid	$\frac{1}{2}$ "
Olive-oil	$2\frac{1}{4}$ "

Shake the bottle well before using. Relief should follow almost immediately.

Colds.

Symptoms.—Chilliness, shivering, languor, dry, hot nose, accompanied by a thin discharge from the nose.

If the patient is not attended to *at once* the complaint may lead to distemper and fevers.

Use Fever Mixture, and keep patient warm.

Colic and Inflammation of the Bowels.

To discover the difference between colic and inflammation of the bowels, press the hand along the belly, and if the movement gives relief, the probable trouble is colic. If pain attends the pressure, it is probably inflammation. In these two cases, my advice is to consult a veterinarian *at once*. The symptoms of both affections are evidenced by the dog standing with arched back and feet drawn toward one another, or crouching with belly on the ground. Inflammation is generally of slower development than colic.

When a dog is affected with colic it is often shown when it is apparently in the best of health and eating well; it is seized with spasms, causing it to moan and howl. The causes are about identical with inflammation of the bowels.

As soon as convinced that colic is the cause of the trouble, give *at once*, to a dog of, say, 25 pounds, *not* quite a teaspoonful of the following in three tablespoonfuls of milk or gruel: compound spirits of sulphuric ether (Hoffman's anodyne) and tincture of opium, *equal parts*. If relief does not immediately ensue, repeat the dose in half an hour.

After permanent relief, give Purgative Mixture, once a day for three days. (See Inflammation of the Bowels.)

COUGHS.

Cough is a symptom of disease rather than a disease in itself, and arises from different causes, differing in character as do the diseases which it precedes, viz.: in the common cold the cough is slight and humid; in bronchitis, hard, dry, and frequent; in inflammation of the lungs and pleurisy, short and suppressed, accompanied with great pain; in asthma, hard and wheezy, followed by vomiting; in distemper, husky and hollow.

For the common cold or cough use either Cough Remedy No. 1 or No. 2. The first is especially good for affections of the respiratory organs.

COUGH REMEDY NO. 1.

Powdered ipecacuanha.	6	grains
" opium.	6	"
Compound squill pill	24	"
Powdered gum ammoniacum	24	"
" licorice	24	"
" rhubarb	12	"

Make into 24 pills. Dose for 25-pound dog, one pill night and morning.

COUGH REMEDY NO. 2.

Elixir paregoric	$\frac{1}{2}$	oz.
Syrup of squills	$1\frac{1}{2}$	"

Give 1 teaspoonful for dog of 25 pounds every six hours.

CUTS, WOUNDS, ETC.

As soon as the cut stops bleeding, which is accomplished either by holding the parts together with the fingers or by use of a lint bandage, wash the wound thoroughly with warm water so as to remove all foreign substances. Then apply with a soft brush a dressing of friars' balsam, which will form a sort of crust over the wound, keeping out dust, dirt, etc., and allowing the wound to heal quickly.

The sewing up of a wound is a very easy affair. Pass the needle through the skin on one side of the wound from the *outside* inward. and through the corresponding part on the opposite side from the *inside* outward. Draw the lips of the wound together gently, and tying the silk thread in a strong knot, cut off ends close, so that the dog cannot bite them. Each stitch must be tied *separately*, and should be about half an inch apart. If possible the dog should be muzzled, not only during the operation, but for several days afterward. The wound should be constantly washed with the following:

Carbolic acid	½ oz.
Glycerin	2 "
Water	32 "

In bandaging a wound, saturate the cloth with a mixture of equal parts of camphorated oil and friars' balsam.

DIARRHEA MIXTURE.

Powdered chalk	3 drams
Aromatic confection (powder)	2 "
Powdered gum acacia	1 dram
Tinct. opium	1 oz.
Oil cassia	8 drops
Tinct. catechu	3 drams
Sp. sal volatile	2 "
Water sufficient to make 8 oz.	

Dose for a young puppy of the *small* breeds, ½ teaspoonful; 1 teaspoonful for puppies of the *large* breeds, and 1 to 2 tablespoonfuls for grown dogs, according to size of the breed. Repeat every three or four hours till relief is obtained or till purging ceases.

DISTEMPER.

There are three kinds of distemper, viz., of the head, of the lungs, and of the bowels. Good nursing is nine points out of ten for conquering this fell disease.

SYMPTOMS.—Mucous discharge from eyes or nose, or both, dry, hacking cough, general lassitude, diarrhea of very offensive odor.

Do not try to treat the patient, for, unless you are an M.D. or have had a long experience with the disease, you will probably make a sorry mess of it. Until a veterinarian arrives, keep the patient quiet, warm, out of all draft, feeding only beef-tea with brandy added. Do not give solid food under any circumstances. Bear always in mind that this disease is most contagious, and, to prevent it from spreading, the patient should be quarantined from all other dogs, the farther off the better.

Dr. T. G. Sherwood, a member of the Royal College of Veterinary Surgery, 127 West Thirty-seventh Street, New York, inoculated four of the author's dogs, and the result was satisfactory beyond all expectation, as other dogs not so treated quickly succumbed to the disease.

As distemper is about equivalent to pneumonia or inflammation of the lungs in human beings, the reader will readily understand how useless it would be for a layman to try to treat these diseases.

Fever Mixture.

Powdered nitre	1 dram
Sweet sp. nitre	½ oz.
Mindererus spirits	1½ "
Wine antimony	1 dram
Water (distilled)	4 oz.

Dose for 25-pound dog, 1 tablespoonful every four hours in a little gruel.

Inflammation of the Bowels.

The main causes of this affection are irregular, improper, or stale diet, irritation caused by some hard, indigestible substance in the stomach, exposure to cold or wet, and a blow, such as a kick.

Symptoms.—Feverishness, nose hot and dry, shivering, distended belly, and scanty or highly colored urine. As this sickness needs scientific treatment, call in a veterinarian *at once*. If, however, you desire to try to relieve the dog awaiting his advent, proceed at once to give injections of thin oatmeal gruel or soap and lukewarm water, each containing about one ounce of castor-oil. Continue these injections every fifteen minutes till relief is given. The utmost gentleness must be used in this procedure, the patient being coaxed to rest on its side while the injections are being administered.

In order to prevent a recurrence of the trouble, give the Mild Purgative No. 1, and after the danger is past, then Tonic Pills No. 1. (See Colic.)

Inflammation of the Bladder.

Use Fever Mixture, preceded by Mild Purgative No. 1.

Lotion for Eyes.

Extract belladonna	½ dram
Rose-water	4 oz.
Wine opium	2 drams

℞ and use as a lotion.

In affections of long standing use:

Sulphite of zinc	. . . . .	12 grains
Tinct. belladonna	. . . . .	1 dram
Wine opium	. . . . .	2 drams
Rose-water	. . . . .	4 oz.

℞ and use as a lotion.

LOTION FOR SORE FEET.

Tinct. arnica	. . . . .	½ oz.
" matico	. . . . .	½ "
" opium	. . . . .	1 "
Acetic acid .	. . . . .	½ "

Mix with 1 quart distilled water and apply freely.

Where inflammation is very great and the feet are swollen, first apply a poultice of bran and boiled turnips, equal parts.

MANGE.

Mange as applied to animals is the same as itch in human beings, being beyond question caused by a parasite burrowing into the skin, resulting in the falling out of the hair, and sometimes in an exudation of an offensive-smelling pus, itching to such a degree that the patient scratches continuously.

There are two varieties of mange, viz., sarcoptic and follicular, both of which are contagious to animals, though very rarely to human beings. The first variety shows itself in little red spots, which exude a sort of pus, and these will spread over the entire body unless checked. Follicular mange is less irritating than the sarcoptic, but gives off a very offensive pus. This variety is generally very stubborn before yielding to treatment.

Provided the affected parts are not raw, rub well into the skin (twice daily) for three days a lotion of equal parts of benzine and sweet-oil. This will destroy the parasites. Then for a week apply daily the following, rubbing it well into the skin:

Milk sulphur	. .	½ oz.
Antimony .	. .	½ "
Whale-oil .	. .	½ pint

Purgative Mixture (Mild) should be given twice a week for at least three weeks.

A surfeit often shows itself on a dog, which is sometimes called red mange. This is not due to a parasite, but to overheated blood, resulting either from improper food, want of exercise, fleas, or inoperative digestive organs. Treat this affection as prescribed for mange.

Purgative Mixture No. 1 (Mild).

Syrup buckthorn (pure)	1½ oz.
" white poppies	½ "
Castor-oil	1 "

Dose, 1 tablespoonful every other day for three days for a dog of 20 pounds. (The bottle should be *well* shaken before measuring out the medicine.)

Purgative Mixture No. 2 (Strong).

Podophyllin	6 grains
Comp. ext. colocynth	30 "
Powd. rhubarb	48 "
Ext. henbane	36 "

Mix and make into 24 pills. For a puppy (setter six months old) a half-pill, assisted with a little broth. Repeat about every twelve hours until proper relief is had.

Tonic Pills No. 1.

Quinine	12 grains
Sulp. of iron	18 "
Ext. gentian	24 "
Powd. ginger	18 "

Make this into 12 pills, giving one night and morning. These are particularly good for debility arising from distemper and kindred diseases.

Tonic No. 2.

Disulphate of quinine	12 grains
Tinct. gentian	6 drams
Syrup orange	6 "
Diluted sulphuric acid	10 drops

Mix and give a teaspoonful daily to a pup (setter). Graduate dose in proportion to size of dog.

Worms.

There are three principal worms infesting dogs.

First, the common roundworm, from two to six inches in length, of a pale pink color, very thin like vermicelli, and greatly resembling the common earth- or angleworm. This is the worm most common in puppies, and inhabits the stomach and lower intestines.

Second, the tænia, or tapeworm, made up of white, flat joints (about half an inch long), often of great length, and also inhabiting the small intestines. It is about as thick as very coarse thread. Both extremities of this worm must be removed, else it will grow again.

Third, the pin- or threadworm, inhabiting the lower bowels,

about half an inch in length and of pinkish color. It is apt to cause partial paralysis in puppies, which disappears after the worms are expelled.

More puppies and grown dogs die each year from worms than from *all diseases combined*. Their presence is generally manifested by the coat being dry and staring, dull and devoid of gloss, disturbed sleep very often resulting in fits, appetite capricious, distention of the stomach, breath generally offensive, nose hot and dry, loss of flesh, diarrhea accompanied by mucous discharge, and general irritableness. From an experience of ten years with Glover's Vermifuge for *all kinds of worms*, I have never found anything to equal it, *especially for puppies*, however delicate. Having made it always a point to give my puppies a couple of doses of vermifuge at two and six months of age, whether they show evidences of having worms or not, I have rarely had any further trouble with these pests.

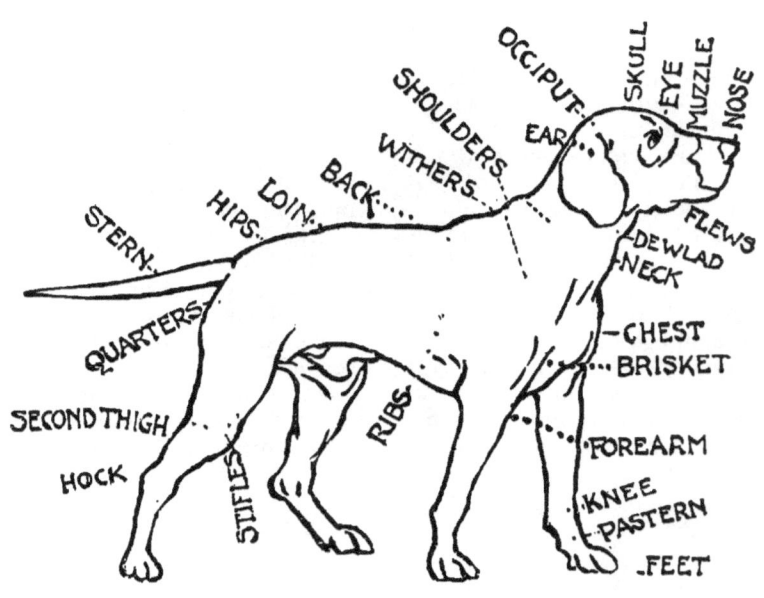

TECHNICAL TERMS.

Apple-head. A rounded head.
Blaze. White mark up the face.
Brisket. The part of the body in front of the chest.
Butterfly-nose. A spotted nose.
Button-ear. An ear whose tip falls over and covers the orifice.
Cat-foot. A round, short foot, like a cat's.
Cheeky. When the dog's cheek-bumps are strongly defined.
Chops. The pendulous lip of the bulldog.
Coat. The hair.
Cobby. Well ribbed up; short and compact body.
Condition. That state of body which shows the coat to be in a healthy state, the bones well covered, the body well rounded, the muscles hard, and the dog in the best of spirits.
Cow-hocked. Hocks which turn in.
Dew-claws. The superfluous claws that often appear above the feet on the inside of the legs.

TECHNICAL TERMS.

Dewlap. Pendulous skin under the throat.
Dish-faced. When the dog's nose is higher than his muzzle at the stop.
Dudley Nose. Flesh-colored.
Elbow. The top joint of the front leg.
Feather. The hair at the back of the legs and under the tail.
Flag. The tail of a setter.
Flews. Pendulous lips, as seen in a bloodhound.
Frill. A mass of hair on the breast.
Harefoot. A long foot, like a hare's.
Haw. The red inside of the eyelid, as shown in bloodhounds, etc.
Height. Measurement taken from top of shoulder to the ground.
Knee. Joint attaching fore pastern and forearm.
Leather. The skin of the ear.
Occiput. The projecting bone or bump at the back of the head.
Overshot. The upper teeth projecting beyond the under.
Pastern. Lowest section of leg, below knee or hock.
Pig-jaw. Same as *overshot*.
Pily. A term applied to a soft, woolly coat next the skin, out of which springs a longer coat.
Prick-ear. One that stands upright.
Quality. Quality is that evidence of breeding which we see in champion dogs, namely, beauty of outline coupled with a fineness of individual points that characterizes the dog at once as being well bred. A horse, for instance, may be very strong and serviceable, yet, being rough and ungainly, is said to be lacking in quality.
Rose-ear. An ear the tip of which turns back and shows the interior of the organ.
Smudge Nose. A nose which is not wholly black, but not spotted, giving the appearance of some of the black having been rubbed off.
Stern. The tail.
Stifles. The top joints of the hind legs.
Stop. The indentation below the eyes, which is most perceptible in the bulldog, but noticeable to a less extent in other breeds.
Trace. Black line extending from occiput to tail.
Tulip-ear. An erect ear.
Type. Every breed of dogs is possessed of certain characteristics of form and feature that stamp it so indelibly that a typical specimen once being seen it is never forgotten. In the human race, for instance, we say a man has a face of Malay type, Chinese type, etc. The same applies to a dog.
Undershot. The lower teeth projecting in front of the upper ones.

BREEDERS' DIRECTORY.

Beagles.
The Wharton Beagles, East Islip, L. I.
Debonair Beagle Kennels, Gloversville, N. Y.

Bulldogs.
C. G. Hopton, Rodney Kennels, Rahway, N. J.
Tyler Morse, Beaverbrook Kennels, North Danvers, Mass.

Collies (Rough).
Brandane Kennels (Black & Hunter), Harrisburg, Pa.
R. G. Steacy, Box 720, Brockville, Ontario.

Great Danes.
C. H. Mantler, Hudson Kennels, 446 Hudson Boulevard, Jersey City Heights, N. J.

Greyhounds.
Woodhaven Kennels, Woodhaven, L. I.
H. M. Nelson, 79 Ninth Street, Long Island City, L. I.
C. M. Higgins, 499 Fourth Street, Brooklyn, N. Y.

Gordon Setters.
J. R. Oughton, Dwight, Ill.

Pomeranians.
Mrs. J. M. Rhodes, Ardmore, Pa.

Poodles (Corded).

S. C. Hodge, 11 Broadway, New York.

Pugs.

Rookery Kennels, 613 Mentor Avenue, Painesville, O.

Russian Wolfhounds.

L. C. Whiton, 114 West Seventy-sixth Street, New York.

St. Bernards (Rough).

Chalkstone Avenue Kennels, 21 Grosvenor Avenue, Providence, R. I.

Setters (English).

Belleplain Kennels, Belleplain, N. J.

Spaniels (Cocker).

Middlesex Kennel, Perth Amboy, N. J.
Edwin W. Fiske, Mount Vernon, N. Y.

Terriers (Black-and-Tan).

Scott Bros., New Cumberland, W. Va.

Terriers (Fox, Smooth).

E. H. Ingroersen, 4144 Prairie Avenue, Chicago, Ill.
William Le Monnier, 833 Union Street, New Orleans, La.

Terriers (Fox, Wire-haired).

A. L. Laukota, Thornelo Kennels, Rochelle Park, New Rochelle, N. Y.

Terriers (Irish).

Irish Terrier Kennels, 352 West Forty-fifth Street, New York.
Huguenot Kennels, New Rochelle, N. Y.

GLOVER'S
Imperial
DOG REMEDIES.

Distemper Cure	price per bottle			$1.00	
Mange Cure	"	"	"	.50	cts.
Vermifuge	"	"	"	.50	"
Tonic	"	"	"	.50	"
Canker Wash	"	"	"	.50	"
Blood Purifier	"	"	"	.50	"
Cough Mixture	"	"	"	.50	"
Eye Lotion	"	"	"	.50	"
Fit Cure	"	"	"	.50	"
Diarrhœa Cure	"	"	"	.50	"
Liniment	"	"	"	.50	"
Worm Capsules	"	"	box	.50	"
Digestive Pills	"	"	"	.50	"
Condition Pills	"	"	"	.50	"
Liver Pills	"	"	"	.50	"
Kennel and Stable Soap	"	"	cake	.25	"

THESE REMEDIES ARE SOLD BY DRUGGISTS
AND DEALERS IN SPORTSMEN'S GOODS.

Book on Dog Diseases and How to Feed
Mailed FREE on application to

H. CLAY GLOVER, VETERINARY SURGEON,

1293 Broadway, New-York.

BOOKS

The following is a list of the MOST DESIRABLE *books pertaining to dogs and their treatment. They will be forwarded to any address on receipt of the price named.*

American Book of the Dog, Shields	$3.50
Bob, The Autobiography of a Fox Terrier	1.50
Book of the Dog, Vero Shaw, with portraits	8.00
Breeders' Kennel Record and Account Book, large 4to	3.00
Diseases of the Dog, Dalziel	80
Dog in Health and Disease, Mills	2.25
Dog, The, Dinks, Mayhew and Hutchinson	3.00
Dog Training *vs.* Breaking, Hammond	1.00
Dogs for Ladies as Companions, Stables	2.00
Dogs of Great Britain and America	2.00
Dogs, Management of, Mayhew, 16mo	75
Dogs, Their Treatment in Disease, "Ashmont"	2.00
Fetch and Carry, Waters	1.00
Glover's Album, Treatise on Canine Diseases	50
Greyhound, Coursing, Breeding and Training, Dalziel	1.00
House and Pet Dogs, illustrated	50
Kennel Secrets, "Ashmont"	3.00
Modern Dogs, Sporting Division, Lee	6.00
Modern Dogs, Non-Sporting Division, Lee	5.00
Modern Dogs, Terriers' Division, Lee	5.00
Modern Training, Waters	2.00
My Dog and I, Huntington	1.00
Our Prize Dogs, Mason	3.00
Pocket Kennel Record, full leather	50
Practical Kennel Guide, Stables, cloth	1.50
Spaniel and its Training, Mercer	1.00
Stonehenge on the Dog, with portraits	2.50
Training Trick Dogs, illustrated, paper	25
Whippet and Race Dog, How to Breed and Race	1.50

BOOKS

In addition, there will be sent free on application a complete Catalogue of all books treating upon the following subjects:

    Adventures (of sportsmen).
    Angling.
    Boating (building canoes, rowboats, etc.).
    Camping (how to build camps, etc.).
    Cats (how to judge, etc.).
    Dogs.
    Ferrets (how to breed, use, etc.).
    Fishing (making flies, rods, etc.).
    Game Laws (all States).
    Games (rules of golf, etc.).
    Guide-books (for hunters and fishermen).
    Guns (how to select, etc.).
    Horses.
    Hunting (large and small game).
    Maps (of lakes and mountains).
    Natural History (birds, butterflies, animals, etc.).
    Shooting (trap, field, etc.).
    Sports (boxing, fencing, etc.).
    Taxidermy (how to stuff game, etc.).
    Trapping (game and birds).
    Yachting (how to build, sail yachts, etc.).
    Yacht Pictures.

        Address

H. W. HUNTINGTON,

NEW YORK CITY.

Can we add just a word to this valuable book, by saying that the very latest modern discovery relating to the COMFORT, HEALTH, and good care of *Dogs*, *Cats*, other animals, *Poultry* and *Plants* is the

P. D. Q.

Powder, which kills *instantly* all Fleas, Lice, other Vermin, and their nits; heals sores; CURES MANGE and slicks up the coat, and overcomes the "dog odor"; saves all washing with strong carbolic soaps or other substances which are *Dangerous* and ruin the hair, and is also the best *Disinfectant* to use in Kennels, Stables, Hen-houses, etc. The P. D. Q. is guaranteed *Non-Explosive and not Poisonous,* even if taken internally by mistake. Has been thoroughly tested and indorsed by the leading dog breeders and papers of the country, among whom are the following: H. W. Huntington, N. Y., President of National Greyhound Club of America; H. W. Lacy, Editor of the *American Stockkeeper*, Boston; J. F. Johnson, K. E., of the *Turf, Field and Farm*, N. Y.; Jas. L. Little, Boston, Secretary of N. E. Kennel Club; Al. G. Eberhart, and many others. The P. D. Q. is for sale by nearly all the Dog and Poultry Supply Stores and Druggists, or can be had from us direct. The retail prices are 1-pound box, 25 cents; 5-pound bags, $1.00, F. O. B., Worcester. The express charges average about 1 cent per ounce additional. Liberal terms to the trade. Write for prices, testimonials, etc.

WORCESTER COMPOUND CO.,
WORCESTER, MASS.

P. O. Box 749.

(Begin at R and read both ways.)

IT IS A MONTHLY MAGAZINE DEVOTED TO EVERYTHING THE NAME IMPLIES.

$1.00 A YEAR.   10C. A COPY.

G. O. SHIELDS (COQUINA).

EDITOR AND MANAGER.

19 W. 24TH STREET, NEW YORK.

TELEPHONE 1427 — 18th ST.

RECREATION prints charming stories of the Fields, the Forests, the Mountains, the Waters.

It prints reminiscences of adventures in many lands.

It tells delightful Camp Fire stories.

It deals with cycling; with natural history; with travel; with yachting, etc.

IDA SIMMONS.

It prints short stories, serials, and scientific articles of general interest.

It gives, each month, one or more full-page pictures of hunting or fishing scenes, any one of which is worth many times the price of a year's subscription. It gives also many smaller views that are beautiful and instructive.

STRIDEAWAY.

A bound volume of RECREATION is a rare panorama of the Chase, and of Out-door Life, in general. No man who loves the rifle, the gun, the rod, the wheel, the woods, the mountains, the waters, the prairies, should try to live without RECREATION.

Send 10 cents for a sample copy.

❁ AT STUD ❁

First Prize Corded Poodle Dog

BLACK PRINCE

A. K. C. S. B. 39424.

Mr. Hodge begs to announce that he has recently imported a magnificent Corded Poodle Bitch, registered in England and America, and descended from both the world-famous dogs, Champions Lyris and Achilles. He expects to soon offer the finest bred Corded Poodle puppies in America.

Address S. C. HODGE,
No. 11 Broadway, New York.

At Stud.

THE TYPICAL BULL DOG

"Beaver Brook Sultan" (formerly "Rustic Sultan"), winner of sixty first and special prizes in England, and winner of first prizes at Montreal, Providence, Mineola and Danbury, 1896.

Fee $30

ADDRESS
TYLER MORSE, } Beaver Brook Kennels, North Danvers, Mass.

FOR SALE: Dogs and Bitches of Pedigree Stock.

TRIANON KENNELS

AT STUD.

THE CELEBRATED

Smooth Fox Terrier "**Prisoner,**"

winner of numerous first and special prizes in England, Canada, and the United States. For Catalog, Stud Cards, etc., address

B. S. HORNE, PITTSBURG, PA.

RUSSIAN WOLFHOUND
"OPTIMIST"

A typical specimen of his class. First Prize Winner in six shows in 1896.

For picture see page 42 of this book.

AT STUD—PUPPIES FOR SALE

Address Owner,

> GEORGE M. KEASBEY,
> 26 Stratford Place, Newark, N. J.

· ENGLISH · SETTERS ·

Gentlemen's Shooting Dogs a Specialty. Broken, Unbroken Dogs, and Puppies, also Brood Bitches.

Any one about to purchase a gentleman's shooting dog is requested to visit BELLEPLAIN and shoot over these dogs until suited.

KENT RODERIGO at Stud. A. K. C. 42253. Vol. 13.

BELLEPLAIN KENNELS,
Belleplain, N. J.

DR. J. T. KENT,
Proprietor.

JOSEPH MASON,
Superintendent.

The American Pet Dog Kennel.

IMPORTER AND BREEDER OF

SMALL PET DOGS,

No. 278 West Eleventh Street, New-York, N. Y.

The Oldest and Most Successful Breeder and Exhibitor in America.

A Specialty in all kinds of

LADIES' PET DOGS.

KING CHARLES SPANIELS,

BLENHEIM SPANIELS,

PRINCE CHARLES SPANIELS,

RUBY SPANIELS.

The Celebrated Champion Romeo — Shortest faced King Charles Spaniel living

Constantly on hand the largest stock of

Japanese Spaniels,

YORKSHIRE TERRIERS, with the longest of coats, from 3 to 6 pounds in weight.

MALTESE TERRIERS,

BLACK AND TAN, of the smallest breed.

PUGS,

MINOTAUR BRED POMERANIANS, Black, White, Chocolate.

DOGS IN THE STUD.

KING CHARLES SPANIEL.

CHAMPION ROMEO (9230),
Beat "King of the Charlies," who was never before beaten.

OLD GOLD (27,116).
(The Ruby Spaniel, one of the best dogs in the Stud.)

JAPANESE SPANIEL — MARU.
Beautifully Coated.
Weight, five pounds.

YORKSHIRE TERRIERS.

HARBORO SWELL.
Weight, five pounds; twenty-six inches of coat.

TED.
Weight, five pounds; fifteen inches of coat.

Mrs. F. Senn, Prop.

Harboro Swell II.

EXCELSIOR
Meat Cakes, Fish Cakes, Hound Meal, Bulldog Meal.

Since the Belfast Dog Show in 1891, when I got the first consignment of your "EXCELSIOR HOUND MEAL," I have used no other kind; before that time my dogs were much troubled with a skin disease brought to my Kennels by a dog from Newcastle-on-Tyne, but in less than three months they were completely free from the disease, and it has not since returned.

My dogs all like the "MEAL," and I find that Puppies fed on it thrive better than on some of the *much puffed* Puppy Foods.

A careful "chemical analysis," made before using it exclusively, proved that the essential and accessory food constituents were present in proper proportions.

I always recommend it to anyone who consults me on the subject.

The Irish "Collie King."

Very truly yours,
(Signed) ROBERT BARKLIE, F.C.S., M.R.I.A., etc.
Consulting and Analytical Chemist.

SWISS MOUNTAIN KENNELS,
GERMANTOWN, PA.

Gentlemen: I have used EXCELSIOR Biscuits now for about five years, and find them perfectly satisfactory in all respects. The dogs are not only fond of them, but even when used exclusively have always agreed splendidly with them, keeping them generally in a good healthy trim. (Signed)
Mrs. F. SMYTH.

"REAL ENGLISH" BOARDING KENNELS,
CLOSTER, N. J.

I have used EXCELSIOR Dog Cakes for twenty years, and five times that number of tons of them, but I must say that the Fish Cakes you are now selling me are the grandest thing for a change of feed that I have ever used.
Yours truly
(Signed),
JOHN BRETT.

RODNEY KENNELS,
RAHWAY, N. J.

I have used about a ton of your EXCELSIOR BULLDOG MEAL with such gratifying results that I take pleasure in sending you this testimony.

Its equal cannot be found for giving coat and condition to *all smooth-coated dogs*. It is a wonderful bone and muscle producer for puppies, and their diet need never be changed from this meal.
(Signed) CHAS. G. HOPTON,
Secretary, Bulldog Club.

FRANKLIN HALLET & CO.
2 and 4 Stone Street,   New York.

Russian Wolfhounds ❧

✳ AT STUD. ✳

IWAN,
By Patrach. Sascza.

PRINCE GALITZIN,
A. K. C. S. B., 41,978,
By Sorvanets-Raskeda.

MY DOGS,

during 1896, have won first and special prizes at Boston, New York, Brooklyn, Providence, Danbury, and Mineola.

Grown dogs and puppies for sale.

WM. L. ANDRUS,
Hudson Terrace,
Yonkers, N. Y.

YOU ARE INVITED

To send for a FREE copy of "GAMELAND," a monthly magazine devoted to outdoor sports. It has been aptly termed "a monthly echo from the woods, the waters, the mountains, and the fields." To the younger generation of sportsmen, it is both instructive and entertaining; to the veteran, it serves as a means for passing pleasantly many an idle hour.

Subscription price, $1.00 per year.   Three trial numbers, 25 cents.

GAMELAND PUBLISHING COMPANY,

03 Rutgers Slip.   INCORPORATED.   New York, N. Y.

USED IN THE KENNEL, IT ABSOLUTELY DESTROYS FLEAS, LICE, AND ALL VERMIN, AND CURES MANGE AND ECZEMA.

ABSOLUTELY PURE. NON-POISONOUS.

Glenrose Dog & Stable Soap,

MANUFACTURED BY

F. W. CHAPMAN,

SOAP MAKER AND PERFUMER,

ANTISEPTIC. SOOTHING.

Sample cake by mail, 25 cents.   ELLSWORTH, MAINE.

USED IN THE STABLE IT CURES SCRATCHES, CUTS, GALLS, AND WOUNDS. CONTAINS *NO* CARBOLIC ACID OR OTHER POISON.

AT   STUD.

"SQUANTO," winner of 1st Prize, Boston; 1st Prize, Mineola.
"HIS NIBS," winner of 1st Prize, Providence; 1st Prize, B'klyn.

Fee $15.00.

A FEW FIRST-CLASS YOUNGSTERS FOR SALE.

ELITE KENNELS,

W. J. BURKART, 1301 Broadway, Brooklyn, N. Y.

JAPANESE ✹ ✹ ✹ ✹

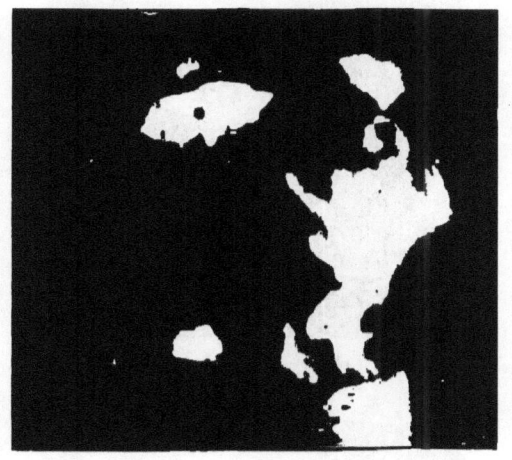

✹ ✹ ✹ ✹ SPANIELS.

AT STUD, JINGO.

FIRST PRIZE WINNER, New York, 1896. Longest Coated Japanese Spaniel in America; weight 4 pounds. **Fee, $25.** Superior Dogs and Puppies for sale at all times.

The Beaumaris Kennels.

"LORD YARMOUTH."

BOSTON TERRIER "RUTH."

"HEATHEN II."   "HEATHEN I."

Manchester, Mass.   Bulkeley Wells, Prop.

Highly Pedigreed

 Boston Terriers and
 English Bull Dogs.

Photographs of Puppies and Full Grown Stock for sale sent to any address on receipt of stamp to cover postage.

STUD CARDS ON APPLICATION.

Winter Address,   Jamaica Plain, Mass.

Founded 1814.

DUMINY & CO.
CHAMPAGNES.

Ship Only One Quality, but two styles of Dryness.

EXTRA QUALITY BRUT
(a strictly natural wine).
1892.

EXTRA QUALITY DRY
(an extremely dry wine).
1892.

♣ ♣ ♣ ♣

THESE WINES HAVE HELD FOR MANY YEARS
THE HIGHEST REPUTATION IN ENGLAND.

Quarts, . . $32.00 per case.
Pints, . . . 34.00 "   "

GREER'S O V H
and Extra Special Liqueur.
Scotch Whiskies.

Antediluvian PURE RYE WHISKIES.

Gold Medals and Awards, Paris, 1889; Jamaica, 1891;
Chicago, 1893; Antwerp, 1894; Bordeaux, 1895.

♣ ♣ ♣ ♣

JOHN OSBORN'S SONS & CO.
Beaver and Broad Sts., New-York.

The Celebrated Stud Greyhound

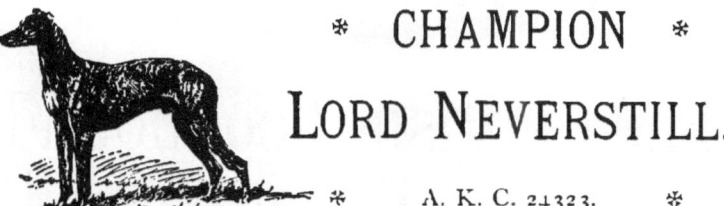

✻ CHAMPION ✻
Lord Neverstill.

✻ A. K. C. 24323. ✻

WINNING.	1st Prize, Chicago, '91; Chicago, '92; Denver, '92; Brooklyn, '92; 1st Challenge, Baltimore, '93; Elmira, '93; Philadelphia, '96; Mineola, '96; Boston, '97; and Champion Prize, Boston, '97; also 15 special prizes.
BREEDING.	Lord Neverstill was whelped April 28th, 1889; breeder, H. C. Lowe of Kansas by his imported Lord Neversettle out of his imported Partera, and is descended from both Contango and Coomassie.

His brothers and sisters have also made for themselves remarkable names in the West on account of their running qualities, among which we find **LIBERTY**, winner of the **National Coursing Derby, 1890. LITTLE CLIMBER, dividing the Hutchinson Coursing Sweepstakes. PRINCE CHARLEY**, winning the **International Stakes, the Columbus Cup, 1893,** his sister **NANCY being second,** and another sister, **PRINCESS MAY, winning the Plate.**

"Lord Neverstill won easily in open dogs and is a cracker; he is well made all over: he has what so few of our greyhounds have — substance and size — his quarters and back are grand and he should run well and get runners."
— *Forest and Stream.*

Address WOODHAVEN KENNELS,
Times Building, New York City.

AT STUD—FEE, $50.

The English Bloodhound Simon de Sudbury
(39095)

Bears an unbeaten record, and acknowledged by the press to be the best Bloodhound in the States.

SIMON DE SUDBURY is 1st prize winner at shows held under A. K. C. Rules, and this offers a grand opportunity for breeders to introduce the best blood at a reasonable price, and should be taken advantage of by all who are interested in the improvement of the breed. Special terms to owners breeding two or more bitches. Mastiffs, St. Bernards, and English Bloodhounds always on sale. For particulars, apply

DR. C. A. LOUGEST,
313 COLUMBUS AVENUE,
BOSTON, MASS.

❀ ENGLISH MASTIFFS ❀

At Stud — Fee $50.00.

BLACK PRINCE BRAMPTON (35,054)
Whelped May, 1894, by Ch. Beaufort's Black Prince ex Ch. Brampton Beauty.

At Stud — Fee $25.00.

RAB L. (28,598)
Whelped Nov., 1893, by Ch. Beaufort's Black Prince ex Winchell's Bess.

EMPEROR WILLIAM (27,271)
A Great Prize Winner.

❀ ST. BERNARDS ❀

At Stud — Fee $25.00.　　　　　Rough-Coated.

SCOTTISH CHIEF (31,979)
Whelped June, 1893, by Scottish Leader (23,958) ex Jess Bedivere, by Ch. Sir Bedivere. He stands 33½ inches high at shoulder, has a grand head, perfectly marked, with even white nose band and blaze, and a dense black shading on face and ears, good neck and body, with immense bone.

At Stud — Fee $15.00.　　　　　Smooth-Coated.

NICODE (33,234)
Whelped Aug., 1893, by Ch. Altoneer ex Ch. Judith.

Exhibitors should avail themselves of the opportunity to secure puppies of the above stock, and no better blood is obtainable in Europe or America. Proof: My winnings at the leading shows 1895, New-York, Boston, Toronto, Can., Providence, R. I., and Danbury, Conn., were 34 first prizes, 22 second prizes and 7 third prizes, including special and kennel prizes at all of the above shows.

For particulars and stud cards apply to

DR. C. A. LOUGEST,
313 Columbus Ave., Boston, Mass.

Dr. T. G. Sherwood

has a well-equipped

❊ Hospital ❊

for the reception of

❊ Sick Dogs, ❊

At 107 W. 37th St., New York.

Telephone, 1363, 38th Street.

Mr. H. W. Huntington

the author of "My Dog and I," being in touch with all the prominent breeders of dogs in the United States, and having officiated as judge at the

Westminster Kennel Club
Metropolitan Kennel Club

and other dog shows, is prepared to accept commissions for the purchase of all breeds of dogs. The benefit of his experience of over twenty years as a successful breeder and exhibitor will be cheerfully given to the prospective buyer.

>Address
>5 West 39th St.,
>New York City.

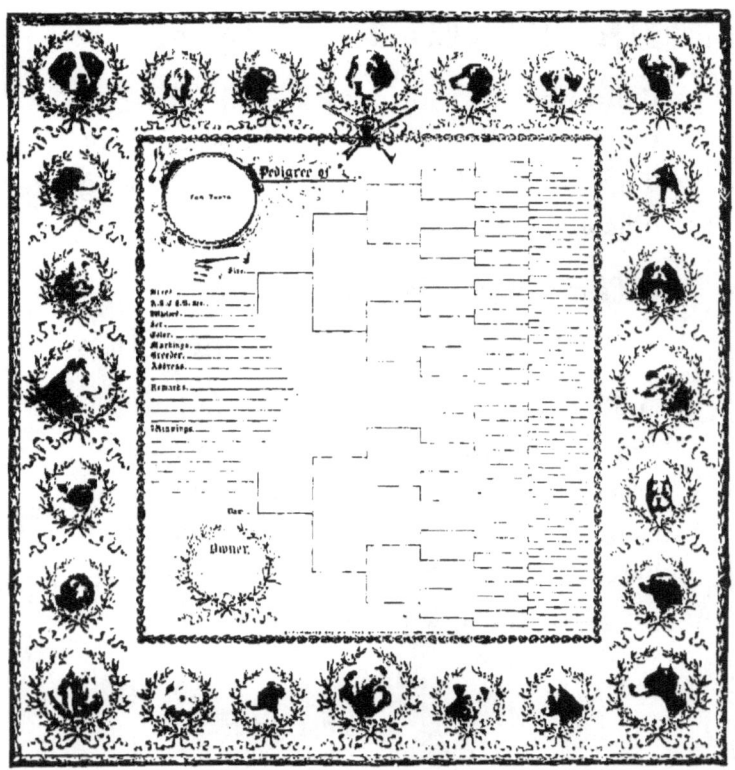

PEDIGREE.

The above is a miniature of the most artistic pedigree blank ever offered to a dog-loving public. The original is complete to the fifth generation, and the whole measures 20 x 21 ½ inches, being printed on the finest paper, with the illustrations in toned colors. Properly framed, it is handsome enough to adorn any wall. Price by mail, $1.00.

EDW. KNIERIEM,
Room No. 7. 112 W. 40th Street. New York City.

www.ingramcontent.com/pod-product-compliance
Lightning Source LLC
Chambersburg PA
CBHW030257170426
43202CB00009B/776